D0482663

A Christmas Treasury

Twelve Unforgettable Holiday Stories

SCHOLASTIC INC.

New York Toronto London Auckland Sydney
Mexico City New Delhi Hong Kong

Contents

From
The Life and Adventures of Santa Claus

L. Frank Baum

From the creator of The Wizard of Oz *comes the story of Santa Claus. L. Frank Baum took the beloved symbol of Christmas and set him in an imaginative world very much like Oz, filled with Fairies, Knooks, Nymphs, and many other fantastical creatures. He gave the boy Claus an exciting life, growing up in an enchanted forest, and he describes the beginnings of good-hearted Claus's toy making. This selection tells why Claus needs ten reindeer to pull his sledge and why the first stockings were hung, and includes the touching tale of the very first Christmas tree.*

*W*hen you remember that no child, until Santa Claus began his travels, had ever known the pleasure of possessing a toy, you will understand how joy crept into the homes of those who had been favored with a visit from the good man, and how they talked of him day by day in loving tones and were honestly grateful for his kindly deeds. It is true that great warriors and mighty kings and clever scholars of that day were often spoken of by the people; but no one of them was so greatly beloved as Santa Claus, because none other was so unselfish as to devote himself to making others happy. For a generous deed lives longer than a great battle or a king's decree or a scholar's essay, because it spreads and leaves its mark on all nature and endures through many generations.

The bargain made with the Knook Prince changed the plans of Claus for all future time; for, being able to use the reindeer on but one night of each year, he decided to devote all the other days to the manufacture of playthings, and on Christmas Eve to carry them to the children of the world.

But a year's work would, he knew, result in a vast accumulation of toys, so he resolved to build a new sledge that would be larger and stronger and better-fitted for swift travel than his old and clumsy one.

His first act was to visit the Gnome King, with whom he made a bargain to exchange three drums, a trumpet, and two dolls for a pair of fine steel runners, curled beautifully at the ends. For the Gnome King had children of his own, who, living in the hollows under the earth, in mines and caverns, needed something to amuse them.

In three days the steel runners were ready, and when Claus brought the playthings to the Gnome King, his Majesty was so greatly pleased with them that he presented Claus with a string of sweet-toned sleigh-bells, in addition to the runners.

"These will please Glossie and Flossie," said Claus, as he jingled the bells and listened to their merry sound. "But I should have two strings of bells, one for each deer."

"Bring me another trumpet and a toy cat," replied the King, "and you shall have a second string of bells like the first."

"It is a bargain!" cried Claus and he went home again for the toys.

The new sledge was carefully built, the Knooks bringing plenty of strong but thin boards to use in its construction. Claus made a high, rounding dash-board to keep off the snow cast behind the fleet hoofs of the deer; and he made high sides to the platform so that many toys could be carried, and finally he mounted the sledge upon the slender steel runners made by the Gnome King.

It was certainly a handsome sledge, and big and roomy. Claus painted it in bright colors, although no one was likely to see it during his midnight journeys, and when all was finished he sent for Glossie and Flossie to come and look at it.

The deer admired the sledge, but gravely declared it was too big and heavy for them to draw.

"We might pull it over the snow, to be sure," said Glossie; "but we could not pull it fast enough to enable us to visit the far-away cities and villages and return to the Forest by daybreak."

"Then I must add two more deer to my team," declared Claus, after a moment's thought.

"The Knook Prince allowed you as many as ten. Why not use them all?" asked Flossie. "Then we could speed like the lightning and leap to the highest roofs with ease."

"A team of ten reindeer!" cried Claus, delightedly. "That will be splendid. Please return to the Forest at once and select eight other deer as like yourselves as possible. And you must all eat of the casa plant, to become strong, and of the grawle plant, to become fleet of foot, and of the marbon plant, that you may live long to accompany me on my journeys. Likewise it will be well for you to bathe in the Pool of Nares, which the lovely Queen Zurline declares will render you rarely beautiful. Should you perform these duties faithfully there is no doubt that on next Christmas Eve my ten reindeer will be the most powerful and beautiful steeds the world has ever seen!"

So Glossie and Flossie went to the Forest to choose their mates, and Claus began to consider the question of a harness for them all.

In the end he called upon Peter Knook for assistance, for Peter's heart is as kind as his body is crooked, and he is remarkably shrewd, as well. And Peter agreed to furnish strips of tough leather for the harness.

This leather was cut from the skins of lions that had reached such an advanced age that they died naturally, and on one side was tawny hair while the other side was cured to the softness of velvet by the deft Knooks. When Claus received these strips of leather he sewed them neatly into a harness for the ten reindeer, and it proved strong and serviceable and lasted him for many years.

The harness and sledge were prepared at odd times, for Claus devoted most of his days to the making of toys. These were now much better than his first ones had been, for the immortals often came to his house to watch him work and to offer suggestions. It was Necile's idea to make some of the dolls say "papa" and "mama." It was a thought of the Knooks to put a squeak inside the lambs, so that when a child squeezed them they would say "baa-a-a-a!" And the Fairy Queen advised Claus to put whistles in the birds, so they could be made to sing, and wheels on the horses, so children could draw them around. Many animals perished in the Forest, from one cause or another, and their fur was brought to Claus that he might cover with it the small images of beasts he made for playthings. A merry Ryl suggested that Claus make a donkey with a nodding head, which he did, and afterward found that it amused the little ones immensely. And so the toys grew in beauty and attractiveness every day, until they were the wonder of even the immortals.

When another Christmas Eve drew near there was a monster load of beautiful gifts for the children ready to be loaded upon the big sledge. Claus filled three sacks to the brim, and tucked every corner of the sledge-box full of toys besides.

Then, at twilight, the ten reindeer appeared and Flossie introduced them all to Claus. They were Racer and Pacer, Reckless and Speckless, Fearless and Peerless, and Ready and Steady, who, with Glossie and Flossie, made up the ten who have traversed the world these hundreds of years with their generous master. They were all exceedingly beautiful, with slender limbs, spreading antlers, velvety dark eyes, and smooth coats of fawn color spotted with white.

7

Claus loved them at once, and has loved them ever since, for they are loyal friends and have rendered him priceless service.

The new harness fitted them nicely and soon they were all fastened to the sledge by twos, with Glossie and Flossie in the lead. These wore the strings of sleigh-bells, and were so delighted with the music they made that they kept prancing up and down to make the bells ring.

Claus now seated himself in the sledge, drew a warm robe over his knees and his fur cap over his ears, and cracked his long whip as a signal to start.

Instantly the ten leaped forward and were away like the wind, while jolly Claus laughed gleefully to see them run and shouted a song in his big, hearty voice:

"With a ho, ho, ho!
And a ha, ha, ha!
And a ho, ho, ha, ha, hee!
Now away we go
O'er the frozen snow,
As merry as we can be!

There are many joys
In our load of toys,
As many a child will know;
We'll scatter them wide
On our wild night ride
O'er the crisp and sparkling snow!"

Now it was on this same Christmas Eve that little Margot and her brother Dick and her cousins Ned and Sara, who were visiting at Margot's house, came in from making a snow man, with their clothes damp, their mittens dripping, and their shoes and stockings wet through and through. They were not scolded, for Margot's mother knew the snow was melting, but they were sent early to bed that their clothes might be hung over chairs to dry. The shoes were placed on the red tiles of the hearth, where the heat from the hot embers would strike them, and the stockings were carefully hung in a row by the chimney, directly over the fireplace. That was the reason Santa Claus noticed them when he came down the chimney that night and all the household were fast asleep. He was in a tremendous hurry and seeing the stockings all belonged to children he quickly stuffed his toys into them and dashed up the chimney again, appearing on the roof so suddenly that the reindeer were astonished at his agility.

"I wish they would all hang up their stockings," he thought, as he drove to the next chimney. "It would save me a lot of time and I could then visit more children before daybreak."

When Margot and Dick and Ned and Sara jumped out of bed the next morning and ran downstairs to get their stockings from the fireplace they were filled with delight to find the toys from Santa Claus inside them. In fact, I think they found more presents in their stockings than any other children of that city had received, for Santa Claus was in a hurry and did not stop to count the toys.

Of course they told all their little friends about it, and of course every one of them decided to hang his own stockings by the fireplace the next Christmas Eve. Even Bessie Blithesome, who made a visit to that city with her father, the great Lord of Lerd, heard the story from the children and hung her own pretty stockings by the chimney when she returned home at Christmas time.

On his next trip Santa Claus found so many stockings hung up in anticipation of his visit that he could fill them in a jiffy and be away again in half the time required to hunt the children up and place the toys by their bedsides.

The custom grew year after year, and has always been a great help to Santa Claus. And, with so many children to visit, he surely needs all the help we are able to give him.

Claus has always kept his promise to the Knooks by returning to the Laughing Valley by daybreak, but only the swiftness of his reindeer has enabled him to do this, for he travels over all the world.

He loved his work and he loved the brisk night ride on his sledge and the gay tinkle of the sleigh-bells. On that first trip with the ten reindeer only Glossie and Flossie wore bells; but each year thereafter for eight years Claus carried presents to the children of the Gnome King, and that good-natured monarch gave him in return a string of bells at each visit, so that finally every one of the ten deer was supplied, and you may imagine what a merry tune the bells played as the sledge sped over the snow.

The children's stockings were so long that it required a great many toys to fill them, and soon Claus found there were other things besides toys that children love. So he sent some of the Fairies, who were always his good friends, into the Tropics, from whence they returned with great bags full of oranges and bananas which they had plucked from the trees. And other Fairies flew to the wonderful Valley of Phunnyland, where delicious candies and bonbons grow thickly on the bushes, and returned laden with many boxes of sweetmeats for the little ones. These things Santa Claus, on each Christmas Eve, placed in the long stockings, together with his toys, and the children were glad to get them, you may be sure.

There are also warm countries where there is no snow in winter, but Claus and his reindeer visited them as well as the colder climes, for there were little wheels inside the runners of his sledge which permitted it to run as smoothly over bare ground as on the snow. And the children who lived in the warm countries learned to know the name of Santa Claus as well as those who lived nearer to the Laughing Valley.

Once, just as the reindeer were ready to start on their

yearly trip, a Fairy came to Claus and told him of three little children who lived beneath a rude tent of skins on a broad plain where there were no trees whatever. These poor babies were miserable and unhappy, for their parents were ignorant people who neglected them sadly. Claus resolved to visit these children before he returned home, and during his ride he picked up the bushy top of a pine tree which the wind had broken off and placed it in his sledge.

It was nearly morning when the deer stopped before the lonely tent of skins where the poor children lay asleep. Claus at once planted the bit of pine tree in the sand and stuck many candles on the branches. Then he hung some of his prettiest toys on the tree, as well as several bags of candies. It did not take long to do all this, for Santa Claus works quickly, and when all was ready he lighted the candles and, thrusting his head in at the opening of the tent, he shouted:

"Merry Christmas, little ones!"

With that he leaped into his sledge and was out of sight before the children, rubbing the sleep from their eyes, could come out to see who had called them.

You can imagine the wonder and joy of those little ones, who had never in their lives known a real pleasure before, when they saw the tree, sparkling with lights that shone brilliant in the gray dawn and hung with toys enough to make them happy for years to come! They joined hands and danced around the tree, shouting and laughing, until they were obliged to pause for breath. And their parents, also, came out to look and wonder, and thereafter had more respect and consideration for their children, since Santa Claus had honored them with such beautiful gifts.

The idea of the Christmas tree pleased Claus, and so the following year he carried many of them in his sledge and set them up in the homes of poor people who seldom saw trees, and placed candles and toys on the branches. Of course he could not carry enough trees in one load for all who wanted them, but in some homes the fathers were able to get trees and have them all ready for Santa Claus when he arrived; and these the good Claus always decorated as prettily as possible and hung with toys enough for all the children who came to see the tree lighted.

These novel ideas and the generous manner in which they were carried out made the children long for that one night in the year when their dear friend Santa Claus should visit them, and as such anticipation is very pleasant and comforting the little ones gleaned much happiness by wondering what would happen when Santa Claus next arrived.

From
Little Women

Louisa May Alcott

This selection from the classic tale tells of the March sisters and their heartwarming Christmas, even without their father. Louisa May Alcott's Little Women *was based on her own childhood in Boston and Concord, Massachusetts. Like the Marches, her parents struggled to raise four young girls. But her father was an influential teacher and counted among his friends Henry David Thoreau, who taught Louisa botany, and Ralph Waldo Emerson, who allowed the young woman use of his extensive library.*

*J*o was the first to wake in the gray dawn of Christmas morning. No stockings hung at the fireplace, and for a moment she felt as much disappointed as she did long ago, when her little sock fell down because it was so crammed with goodies. Then she remembered her mother's promise, and slipping her hand under her pillow, drew out a little crimson-covered book. She knew it very well, for it was that beautiful old story of the best life ever lived, and Jo felt that it was a true guidebook for any pilgrim going the long journey. She woke Meg with a "Merry Christmas," and bade her see what was under her pillow. A green-covered book appeared, with the same picture inside, and a few words written by their mother, which made their one present very precious in their eyes. Presently Beth and Amy woke, to rummage and find their little books also — one dove-colored, the other blue; and all sat looking at and talking about them, while the east grew rosy with the coming day.

In spite of her small vanities, Margaret had a sweet

and pious nature, which unconsciously influenced her sisters, especially Jo, who loved her very tenderly, and obeyed her because her advice was so gently given.

"Girls," said Meg seriously, looking from the tumbled head beside her to the two little nightcapped ones in the room beyond, "Mother wants us to read and love and mind these books, and we must begin at once. We used to be faithful about it, but since Father went away, and all this war trouble unsettled us, we have neglected many things. You can do as you please, but *I* shall keep my book on the table here and read a little every morning as soon as I wake, for I know it will do me good and help me through the day."

Then she opened her new book and began to read. Jo put her arm round her, and, leaning cheek to cheek read also, with the quiet expression so seldom seen on her restless face.

"How good Meg is! Come, Amy, let's do as they do. I'll help you with the hard words, and they'll explain things if we don't understand," whispered Beth, very much impressed by the pretty books and her sisters' example.

"I'm glad mine is blue," said Amy. And then the rooms were very still while the pages were softly turned, and the winter sunshine crept in to touch the bright heads and serious faces with a Christmas greeting.

"Where is Mother?" asked Meg, as she and Jo ran down to thank her for their gifts, half an hour later.

"Goodness only knows. Some poor creeter come

a-beggin', and your ma went straight off to see what was needed. There never *was* such a woman for givin' away vittles and drink, clothes and firin'," replied Hannah, who had lived with the family since Meg was born, and was considered by them all more as a friend than a servant.

"She will be back soon, I think, so fry your cakes, and have everything ready," said Meg, looking over the presents which were collected in a basket and kept under the sofa, ready to be produced at the proper time. "Why, where is Amy's bottle of cologne?" she added, as the little flask did not appear.

"She took it out a minute ago, and went off with it to put a ribbon on it, or some such notion," replied Jo, dancing about the room to take the first stiffness off the new army slippers.

"How nice my handkerchiefs look, don't they? Hannah washed and ironed them for me, and I marked them all myself," said Beth, looking proudly at the somewhat uneven letters which had cost her such labor.

"Bless the child! she's gone and put 'Mother' on them instead of 'M. March.' How funny!" cried Jo, taking up one.

"Isn't it right? I thought it was better to do it so, because Meg's initials are 'M. M.,' and I don't want anyone to use them but Marmee," said Beth, looking troubled.

"It's all right, dear, and a very pretty idea — quite sensible, too, for no one can ever mistake now. It will please her very much, I know," said Meg, with a frown for Jo and a smile for Beth.

"There's Mother. Hide the basket, quick!" cried Jo, as a door slammed, and steps sounded in the hall.

Amy came in hastily, and looked rather abashed when she saw her sisters all waiting for her.

"Where have you been, and what are you hiding behind you?" asked Meg, surprised to see, by her hood and cloak, that lazy Amy had been out so early.

"Don't laugh at me, Jo! I didn't mean anyone should know till the time came. I only meant to change the little bottle for a big one, and I gave *all* my money to get it, and I'm truly trying not to be selfish any more."

As she spoke, Amy showed the handsome flask which replaced the cheap one, and looked so earnest and humble in her little effort to forget herself that Meg hugged her on the spot, and Jo pronounced her "a trump," while Beth ran to the window, and picked her finest rose to ornament the stately bottle.

"You see I felt ashamed of my present, after reading and talking about being good this morning, so I ran round the corner and changed it the minute I was up: and I'm *so* glad, for mine is the handsomest now."

Another bang of the street door sent the basket under the sofa, and the girls to the table, eager for breakfast.

"Merry Christmas, Marmee! Many of them! Thank you for our books; we read some, and mean to every day," they cried, in chorus.

"Merry Christmas, little daughters! I'm glad you began at once, and hope you will keep on. But I want to say one word before we sit down. Not far away from here lies a poor woman with a little newborn baby. Six children are huddled into one bed to keep from freezing, for they have no fire. There is nothing to eat over there, and the oldest boy came to tell me they were suffering hunger and cold. My girls, will you give them your breakfast as a Christmas present?"

They were all unusually hungry, having waited nearly an hour, and for a minute no one spoke — only a minute, for Jo exclaimed impetuously, "I'm so glad you came before we began!"

"May I go and help carry the things to the poor little children?" asked Beth eagerly.

"*I* shall take the cream and the muffins," added Amy, heroically giving up the article she most liked.

Meg was already covering the buckwheats, and piling the bread into one big plate.

"I thought you'd do it," said Mrs. March, smiling as if satisfied. "You shall all go and help me, and when we come back we will have bread and milk for breakfast, and make it up at dinnertime."

They were soon ready, and the procession set out. Fortunately it was early, and they went through back streets, so few people saw them, and no one laughed at the queer party.

A poor, bare, miserable room it was, with broken

21

windows, no fire, ragged bedclothes, a sick mother, wailing baby, and a group of pale, hungry children cuddled under one old quilt, trying to keep warm.

How the big eyes stared and the blue lips smiled as the girls went in!

"*Ach, mein Gott!* It is good angels come to us!" said the poor woman, crying for joy.

"Funny angels in hoods and mittens," said Jo, and set them laughing.

In a few minutes it really did seem as if kind spirits had been at work there. Hannah, who had carried wood, made a fire, and stopped up the broken panes with old hats and her own cloak. Mrs. March gave the mother tea and gruel, and comforted her with promises of help, while she dressed the little baby as tenderly as if it had been her own. The girls, meantime, spread the table, set the children round the fire, and fed them like so many hungry birds — laughing, talking, and trying to understand the funny broken English.

"*Das ist gut!*" "*Die Engel-kinder!*" cried the poor things, as they ate and warmed their purple hands at the comfortable blaze.

The girls had never been called angel children before, and thought it very agreeable, especially Jo, who had been considered a "Sancho" ever since she was born. That was a very happy breakfast, though they didn't get any of it; and when they went away, leaving comfort behind, I think there were not in all the city four merrier people than the hungry little girls who gave away their breakfasts and contented themselves with bread and milk on Christmas morning.

"That's loving our neighbor better than ourselves, and I like it," said Meg, as they set out their presents, while their mother was upstairs collecting clothes for the poor Hummels.

Not a very splendid show, but there was a great deal of love done up in the few little bundles, and the tall vase of red roses, white chrysanthemums, and trailing vines, which stood in the middle, gave quite an elegant air to the table.

"She's coming! Strike up, Beth! Open the door, Amy! Three cheers for Marmee!" cried Jo, prancing about while Meg went to conduct Mother to the seat of honor.

Beth played her gayest march, Amy threw open the door, and Meg enacted escort with great dignity. Mrs. March was both surprised and touched, and smiled with her eyes full as she examined her presents, and read the little notes which accompanied them. The slippers went on at once, a new handkerchief was slipped into her pocket, well scented with Amy's cologne, the rose was fastened in her bosom, and the nice gloves were pronounced a "perfect fit."

There was a good deal of laughing and kissing and explaining, in the simple, loving fashion which makes these home festivals so pleasant at the time, so sweet to remember long afterward, and then all fell to work.

The morning charities and ceremonies took so much time that the rest of the day was devoted to preparations for the evening festivities. Being still too young to go often to the theater, and not rich enough to afford any great outlay for private performances, the girls put their wits to work, and — necessity being the mother of invention — made whatever they needed. Very clever were some of their productions, — pasteboard guitars, antique lamps made of old-fashioned butter boats covered with silver paper, gorgeous robes of old cotton, glittering with tin spangles from a pickle factory, and armor covered with the same useful diamond-shaped bits left in sheets when the lids of tin preserve pots were cut out. The furniture was used to being turned topsy-turvy, and the big chamber was the scene of many innocent revels.

No gentlemen were admitted, so Jo played male parts to her heart's content and took immense satisfaction in a pair of russet-leather boots given her by a friend, who knew a lady who knew an actor. These boots, an old foil, and a slashed doublet once used by an artist for some picture, were Jo's chief treasures, and appeared on all occasions. The smallness of the company made it necessary for the two principal actors to take several parts apiece, and they certainly deserved some credit for the hard work they did in learning three or four different parts, whisking in and out of various costumes, and managing the stage besides. It was excellent drill for their memories, a harmless amusement, and employed many hours which otherwise would have been idle, lonely, or spent in less profitable society.

On Christmas night, a dozen girls piled onto the bed which was the dress circle, and sat before the blue and yellow chintz curtains in a most flattering state of expectancy. There was a good deal of rustling and whispering behind the curtain, a trifle of lamp smoke, and an occasional giggle from Amy, who was apt to get hysterical in the excitement of the moment. Presently a bell sounded, the curtains flew apart, and the *Operatic Tragedy* began.

The excitement had hardly subsided when Hannah appeared, with "Mrs. March's compliments, and would the ladies walk down to supper."

This was a surprise, even to the actors, and when they saw the table, they looked at one another in rapturous amazement. It was like Marmee to get up a little treat for them, but anything so fine as this was unheard of since the departed days of plenty. There was ice cream — actually two dishes of it pink and white — and cake and fruit and distracting French bonbons and, in the middle of the table, four great bouquets of hothouse flowers!

It quite took their breath away; and they stared first

at the table and then at their mother, who looked as if she enjoyed it immensely.

"Is it fairies?" asked Amy.

"It's Santa Claus," said Beth.

"Mother did it." And Meg smiled her sweetest, in spite of her gray beard and white eyebrows.

"Aunt March had a good fit, and sent the supper," cried Jo, with a sudden inspiration.

"All wrong. Old Mr. Laurence sent it," replied Mrs. March.

"The Laurence boy's grandfather! What in the world put such a thing into his head? We don't know him!" exclaimed Meg.

"Hannah told one of his servants about your breakfast party. He is an odd old gentleman, but that pleased him. He knew my father, years ago, and he sent me a polite note this afternoon, saying he hoped I would allow him to express his friendly feeling toward my children by sending them a few trifles in honor of the day. I could not refuse, and so you have a little feast at night to make up for the bread-and-milk breakfast."

"That boy put it into his head, I know he did! He's a capital fellow, and I wish we could get acquainted. He looks as if he'd like to know us but he's bashful, and Meg is so prim she won't let me speak to him when we pass," said Jo, as the plates went round, and the ice began to melt out of sight, with "Ohs!" and "Ahs!" of satisfaction.

"You mean the people who live in the big house next door, don't you?" asked one of the girls. "My mother knows old Mr. Laurence, but says he's very proud and doesn't like to mix with his neighbors. He keeps his grandson shut up, when he isn't riding or walking with his tutor, and makes him study very hard. We invited him to our party, but he didn't come. Mother says he's very nice, though he never speaks to us girls."

"Our cat ran away once, and he brought her back, and we talked over the fence, and were getting on capitally — all about cricket, and so on — when he saw Meg coming, and walked off. I mean to know him some day, for he needs fun, I'm sure he does," said Jo decidedly.

"I like his manners, and he looks like a gentleman; so I've no objection to your knowing him, if a proper opportunity comes. He brought the flowers himself, and I should have asked him in, if I had been sure what was going on upstairs. He looked so wistful as he went away, hearing the frolic and evidently having none of his own."

"It's a mercy you didn't, Mother!" laughed Jo, looking at her boots. "But we'll have another play sometime that he *can* see. Perhaps he'll help act. Wouldn't that be jolly?"

"I never had such a fine bouquet before! How pretty it is!" And Meg examined her flowers with great interest.

"They *are* lovely! But Beth's roses are sweeter to me," said Mrs. March, smelling the half-dead posy in her belt.

Beth nestled up to her, and whispered softly, "I wish I could send a bunch to Father. I'm afraid he isn't having such a merry Christmas as we are."

Yes, Virginia, There Is a Santa Claus

Virginia O'Hanlon and

Francis P. Church

In 1897, a little girl named Virginia O'Hanlon asked her father whether Santa Claus was real. Her father suggested she write to the Question and Answer column in the New York Sun. *Francis P. Church, the editor of the newspaper, printed Virginia's letter and wrote this wonderful response that the* Sun *printed every year until 1949, when the paper went out of business.*

$\mathcal{W}$e take pleasure in answering at once and thus prominently the communication below, expressing at the same time our great gratification that its faithful author is numbered among the friends of the *Sun*.

Dear Editor:
I am 8 years old.
Some of my little friends say there is no Santa Claus.
Papa says "If you see it in 'The Sun' it's so."
Please tell me the truth, is there a Santa Claus?
Virginia O'Hanlon,
115 West 95th Street,
New York City

Virginia, your little friends are wrong. They have been affected by the skepticism of a skeptical age. They do not believe except they see. They think that nothing can be which is not comprehensible by their little minds. All minds, Virginia, whether they be men's or children's, are little. In this great universe of ours man is a mere insect, an ant, in his intellect, as compared with the boundless world about him, as measured by the intelligence capable of grasping the whole of truth and knowledge.

Yes, Virginia, there is a Santa Claus. He exists as certainly as love and generosity and devotion exist, and you know that they abound and give to your life its highest beauty and joy. Alas! how dreary would be the world if there were no Santa Claus! It would be as dreary as if there were no Virginias. There would be no childlike faith, then, no poetry, no romance to make tolerable this existence. We should have no enjoyment, except in sense and sight. The external light with which childhood fills the world would be extinguished.

Not believe in Santa Claus! You might as well not believe in fairies! You might get your papa to hire men to watch in all the chimneys on Christmas Eve to catch Santa Claus, but even if they did not see Santa Claus coming down, what would that prove? Nobody sees Santa Claus, but that is no sign that there is no Santa Claus. The most real things in the world are those that neither children nor men can see. Did you ever see fairies dancing on the lawn? Of course not, but that's no proof that they are not there. Nobody can conceive or imagine all the wonders there are unseen and unseeable in the world.

You tear apart the baby's rattle and see what makes

the noise inside, but there is a veil covering the unseen world which not the strongest man, nor even the united strength of all the strongest men that ever lived, could tear apart. Only faith, poetry, love, romance, can push aside that curtain and view and picture the supernal beauty and glory beyond. Is it all real? Ah, Virginia, in all this world there is nothing else real and abiding.

No Santa Claus! Thank God he lives, and he lives forever. A thousand years from now, Virginia, nay ten times ten thousand years from now, he will continue to make glad the heart of childhood.

Francis P. Church
New York Sun editorial,
September 21, 1897

From
Miracle on 34th Street

A novelization by Todd Strasser. Based on the 1947 motion picture screenplay by George Seaton and story by Valentine Davies. Screenplay by George Seaton and John Hughes

Based on a popular movie first released in 1947, this story has been a staple of Christmas since then. In the 1997 remake, a little girl named Susan and her mother meet a department store Santa who really is Kriss Kringle. When Kriss is made to look bad by Victor Lamberg, the owner of a rival department store, a lawyer named Bryan Bedford defends the jolly old man by reminding everyone of the true spirit of Christmas and what Santa Claus means to all people — young and old.

*T*hursday morning, there was already a large crowd outside the courthouse when Bryan got there. Bryan smiled to himself and went inside. The courtroom was packed with spectators and the press. Since no one knew that he was Kriss's attorney, he was able to get all the way down to the plaintiff's table without being cornered by a reporter.

Last time I'll get away with that, he thought, as he laid his briefcase on the plaintiff's table. He nodded over at Ed Collins at the prosecution table, and Collins nodded back stiffly. Bryan sat down and opened his briefcase. Already, the newspaper sketch artists were busy drawing him.

A moment later the bailiff brought Kriss in from the pens in the back. Kriss was wearing a nice old tweed suit, and he looked around in amazement as the bailiff led him to the chair next to Bryan.

"Hey, Kriss." Bryan tried to act relaxed. He didn't want to make Kriss more nervous than he already was.

"Hello, Bryan," Kriss said, looking around wide-eyed.

"You look like you've never been in court before."

"Well, the truth is, I haven't," Kriss replied.

"Then I'll tell you one thing," Bryan said. "Wherever you go, you attract a crowd. If you think the inside of this courtroom is full, you should see what's going on outside."

"This isn't the way I want people to see me," Kriss said.

"How're they treating you?" Bryan asked.

"Well enough, I suppose," Kriss replied. "But I must say, I'm rather uneasy about this."

"You'll be fine." Bryan patted him gently on the back. "All you have to do is tell the truth."

Kriss looked around some more. Then he leaned toward Bryan and whispered, "Who's the sour-looking fellow in the gray suit?"

"The prosecutor," Bryan whispered back.

"Is there anything I should know about him?" Kriss whispered.

"Yeah," Bryan whispered back. "He doesn't believe in Santa Claus."

"All rise," the bailiff said. Everyone in the courtroom stood up as Judge Harper, wearing black judicial robes, entered from a door in the back.

"That's the judge?" Kriss whispered in surprise.

"Correct," Bryan whispered back.

"Trial term, part three," the bailiff announced. "Justice Harper presiding. All those having business with the court, draw near and you shall be heard."

Edward Collins rose to his feet. "In the matter of Kriss Kringle, Your Honor, the commitment papers are before you. If Your Honor pleases, I should like to call the first witness."

"Go ahead, counselor," Judge Harper replied.

Collins turned to Kriss. "Mr. Kringle, will you please take the stand?"

Kriss glanced nervously at Bryan, who gave him a reassuring wink. He rose slowly and walked toward the witness stand. Then he gave Judge Harper a big smile. "Good morning, Judge, how's Ryan, that grandson of yours?"

Judge Harper did a double take.

"At the Thanksgiving Day parade, remember?" Kriss said in a low voice. "He thought I looked like Santa Claus."

Judge Harper blinked, then looked over at the bailiff, who had come over.

"Do you swear to tell the truth, the whole truth, and nothing but the truth, so help you God?"

Kriss looked around and frowned. "Don't I have to put my hand on a Bible?"

"Not in this court, sir," the bailiff replied.

"Then I'll put it over my heart instead," Kriss said, placing his right hand on his heart. "I do."

Edward Collins stepped out from behind the prosecutor's table and started toward Kriss.

"Ahem." Judge Harper cleared his throat. "Before you begin, Mr. Collins, I want to explain to the witness and all present that this is a hearing, not a trial." He leaned over the bench toward Kriss. "Mr. Kringle, you do not have to answer any questions against your wishes or even testify at all."

"We have no objections, Your Honor," Bryan said.

"I'm in good voice this afternoon," Kriss said cheerfully. "I'll be glad to answer any questions that I can."

"What is your name?" Collins asked.

"Oh, I'm sorry," Kriss said. "I didn't introduce myself. Pardon me. I'm Mr. Kringle. Kriss Kringle."

Titters started to spread through the gallery.

Bang! Judge Harper slammed down his gavel. "Order in the court!"

"You said your name is Kriss Kringle," Collins said.

"With two Ks," Kriss said.

"Where do you live?" Collins asked.

"At the moment I'm residing at Bellevue Hospital," Kriss replied. "It's reasonably comfortable."

Again titters rippled through the crowd. *Bang!* Again the judge slammed down his gavel.

"Mr. Kriss Kringle," Collins said. "Do you believe that you are Santa Claus?"

The question surprised Kriss. "Would I be sitting here if I didn't?"

Judge Harper leaned over the bench. "Please answer with a yes or a no. Do you believe you are Santa Claus?"

"Yes."

The room fell silent. Ed Collins looked a little startled at the forthrightness with which Kriss had answered. Behind the plaintiff's table, Bryan gave Kriss an encouraging thumbs-up sign. Collins collected himself and turned to the judge.

"The state rests, Your Honor," he said. There was a rumble of conversation in the seats behind him as he returned to his seat.

Judge Harper turned to Bryan. "Do you wish to cross-examine the witness?"

"I have no questions at this time," Bryan replied.

"You may step down," the bailiff said to Kriss, who stood up and bowed to the judge.

"It was very nice seeing you again," he said.

Judge Harper once again turned to Bryan. "In view of your client's statement, do you still wish to put on a defense?"

"I do, Your Honor," Bryan replied. "I should like to call my first witness."

From out of the gallery came the little girl named Dorothy who'd asked Kriss for the Patty Polliwog. Kriss smiled when he saw her, and she waved hello. The bailiff put a thick telephone book on the witness's chair, and Dorothy sat down.

"Can you please tell the court your name," Bryan said.

"My name is Dorothy Lowry," she said.

"Thank you, Dorothy," Bryan said. "Now, will you please tell the court what you got for Christmas last year?"

"Um, a dollhouse."

"Who gave you that dollhouse?" Bryan asked.

Dorothy pointed at Kriss. "Him."

"And what is his name?" Bryan asked.

"Santa Claus," Dorothy said.

"Are you sure he's Santa Claus?" Bryan asked.

"Yep."

"How can you be sure?"

"Because he looks like Santa Claus," Dorothy said.

"I see." Bryan rubbed his chin. "Are there any other reasons you think he's Santa?"

"He's very nice," Dorothy said.

Bryan pointed at Edward Collins. "Could that man be Santa?"

"No." Dorothy shook her head.

"Why not?"

"Santa Claus isn't bald."

The courtroom erupted in laughter.

Bang! Judge Harper slammed down his gavel. "Order in the court!"

Collins stood up. "Your Honor, this testimony is ridiculous, irrelevant, and immaterial. Mr. Bedford is making a mockery of these proceedings. It hasn't been established that there is such a person as Santa Claus."

"Your Honor," Bryan quickly replied, "I would ask Mr. Collins if he can offer any proof that there is *no* Santa Claus."

Murmurs broke out in the gallery. For a moment Edward Collins looked completely off guard. But then he must have thought of something, because he quickly turned to Judge Harper.

"Your Honor," he said, "I would like to request a recess until tomorrow so that I might adequately prepare to meet Mr. Bedford's challenge."

Judge Harper turned to Bryan. "Mr. Bedford, do you have any objections?"

"No, Your Honor."

Another murmur spread through the gallery.

Bang! Judge Harper brought the gavel down. "This court stands in recess until nine o'clock tomorrow morning."

Bryan left the courtroom with his head down, deep in thought. A number of reporters were waiting for him, and he paused for a moment.

"Mr. Bedford! Do you really think your client is Santa Claus?" one asked.

"Absolutely," Bryan replied.

"Why?"

"Because no one has proved to me that he isn't," Bryan said.

"Are you worried that Ed Collins is going to do exactly that tomorrow morning?"

"I'd like to see him try," Bryan said with a smile.

As Bryan expected, Collins brought in an expert witness the next morning. Dr. Arthur Hunter, a tweedy professor from Columbia, took the stand. He polished his gold wire-trimmed glasses, and began a very thorough discourse on the history of Santa Claus.

"St. Nicholas, also known as Santa Claus, was a fourth-century bishop of Myra Lycia, Asia Minor," the professor told the packed courtroom. "He was imprisoned during the reign of the Roman emperor Diocletian's persecution of Christians and was released under the rule of Constantine the Great. In the sixth century, Italian sailors brought his body to Bari, Italy. His relics are enshrined in the basilica of St. Nicola, in Bari. His legend is credited with a number of miracles, the best known dealing with saving children from tragedy."

While Kriss looked at Bryan and rolled his eyes, Edward Collins questioned the professor.

"You mentioned miracles," the prosecutor said. "Do you believe in miracles, Dr. Hunter?"

"I believe in fortuitous events," the professor replied.

"But I mean miracles," Collins pressed on. "Extraordinary events in the physical world that surpass all known human or natural powers and are ascribed to supernatural causes."

Dr. Hunter thought for a moment and then replied, "I can't say that I believe in miracles as you have framed the term."

"Dr. Hunter," Collins said, "what is the church's position on St. Nicholas?"

"He's a recognized saint," the professor replied.

"Is it not true that in 1969 his feast day was dropped from the calendar?" the prosecutor asked.

"That's correct."

"So, in essence, the church walked away from St. Nicholas," Collins said. "So would they not also walk away from the diluted, derivative secular figure, Santa Claus?"

"I, uh, would presume so," Dr. Hunter replied.

Collins turned a smug grin toward Kriss and said, "No further questions for this witness."

"Would you like to cross-examine?" Judge Harper asked Bryan.

"No, thank you, Your Honor," Bryan replied.

The prosecution's next witness wore the green uniform of an Air Force Commander. George Colson was a ruggedly handsome man with clipped blond hair.

"Tell me, Commander," Collins said. "Have you ever been to the North Pole?"

"Yes, sir," Colson replied. "In 1972 and again in 1984."

"You explored the region?"

"Extensively."

"Did you ever come across any evidence of dwellings, animal pens, barns, or workshops?" Collins asked.

"No, sir."

"Did you ever come across any evidence of settlements whatsoever?"

"None, sir."

Collins crossed his arms, glancing back at Bryan and Kriss. "In your opinion, Commander, would it be possible for an individual, such as Mr. Kringle, to create a settlement in that inhospitable region large enough to manufacture at least one toy for each of the earth's 1.7 billion children?"

"No, sir," Colson answered.

"No further questions," Collins said.

"Cross-examination?" Judge Harper asked.

"No, thank you, Your Honor," Bryan answered calmly as he made notes on a pad of yellow lined paper.

Suddenly Kriss rose to his feet. "There isn't any way that gentleman could have seen my workshops!" he stated in exasperation. "They're invisible!"

A loud murmur broke out in the courtroom.

Bang! Judge Harper slammed down the gavel. "Order!"

"Kriss!" Bryan hissed, putting his hand on the old man's shoulder. "Sit down, please."

Kriss sat down and leaned toward Bryan. "Mr. Collins is completely mistaken," he whispered. "My workshops don't exist in the physical world. They're in the dream world. I thought this was understood."

"Don't worry," Bryan replied, giving him a reassuring pat on the back. "Let me be the lawyer."

Now the doors at the back of the courtroom opened, and two men led in a large reindeer. A very loud murmur spread through the crowd, and Judge Harper was so surprised he momentarily forgot to use his gavel.

Bang! Bang! Bang! He quickly remembered. "Mr. Collins, what is the meaning of this?"

"This is a reindeer, Your Honor," Collins replied as the creature was brought before the bench.

"I can see that," Judge Harper huffed. "What is it doing in my courtroom?"

"I'd like the court to see if Mr. Kringle can make it fly," Collins replied. He smiled at Kriss.

Kriss smiled back.

Edward Collins stopped smiling. "Mr. Kringle? If you would proceed."

Before Kriss could do anything, Bryan leaned toward him. "He's baiting you," he warned in a low voice. "He wants you to lose your temper. He wants you to act crazy. Remember that."

Kriss stood up. "I would love to oblige you, Mr. Collins, but I cannot make that reindeer fly."

"I thought so," Collins said.

"They only fly on Christmas Eve," Kriss added. "Tomorrow night to be precise."

Laughter burst out of the gallery, but quickly stopped. Collins didn't appear at all surprised by the answer.

"Of course, Mr. Kringle," he said and turned to Judge Harper. "The State of New York certainly has no interest in laying waste to a colorful myth, but this hearing isn't about mythology. It's about the mental competency of a man who believes himself to be a myth. Everyone in this courtroom, if they were entirely honest with themselves, would have to conclude that Mr. Kringle is, regrettably, . . . insane."

Bryan watched uncomfortably as Kriss's hands balled into fists. Noting Kriss's growing agitation, Collins continued.

"As a sworn guardian of the laws of the State of New York, as a citizen, and as a father," he said, "it is my wish that this man, who masquerades as a figure of benevolence and generosity for profit . . ."

Kriss bolted out of his chair. "That is not true!"

"Kriss!" Bryan reached for him. "Sit down, please."

Bang! Judge Harper slammed down the gavel. "Mr. Kringle will refrain from comment, or he will be removed from the courtroom and these proceedings will continue without him. Go on, Mr. Collins."

"It is my wish that Mr. Kringle come under the supervision of the state so that the children of New York

State are not put at risk," Collins said. "No one wants to wait until Mr. Kringle injures a child before we act."

Kriss instantly started to rise. Bryan placed his hand on his shoulder to stop him, but the man slapped his hand away. Suddenly, a child's voice rang out through the courtroom.

"Hey, you big jerk!"

Bryan quickly looked around and saw Susan standing on her seat. He'd thought the voice sounded familiar.

"Mr. Kringle's the nicest person in the world!" Susan shouted. "He'd never hurt anybody!"

Bang! Bang! Bang! Judge Harper wielded the gavel. "Order! Order, I said!"

Luckily for Bryan, Susan's outburst took the sting out of Collins's words about Kriss. The old man smiled at Susan. This time, when Bryan put his hand on his shoulder, Kriss let himself be pulled back down.

"We're almost through, Kriss." Bryan tried again to reassure him. "Sit down and relax. It's going to be okay."

Bang! Bang! Bang! Judge Harper had to bang his gavel a few more times before order was restored. "Do you wish to continue, Mr. Collins?"

"No, Your Honor. The state rests."

As Collins returned to his seat, Bryan leaned over and winked at him. "Thanks."

Collins frowned as if he didn't understand.

"I had nothing," Bryan whispered. "My only defense was your offense."

Collins gave Bryan a look like he was crazy. Bryan wasn't surprised. The prosecutor still didn't get it.

"Mr. Bedford, have you anything to say?" Judge Harper asked.

"No, Your Honor," Bryan said, once again snapping his briefcase closed. "I have no further witnesses. I rest my case."

Judge Harper looked surprised. "Very well, then, I shall render my opinion on this matter at twelve o'clock noon, tomorrow. Until that time, this court is in recess."

Bang! He slammed down the gavel.

Once again, Kriss was taken back to Bellevue, and Bryan stepped out of the court and was surrounded by reporters.

"Mr. Bedford, why didn't you present a stronger case for your client?"

"I didn't have to," Bryan replied.

"Do you really think Kriss Kringle has a chance?"

"He wouldn't be Santa Claus if he didn't."

The reporters chuckled at that one.

"How does it feel to have to wait another day?" asked another reporter.

"Oh, it's all right," Bryan said. "Somehow I think it's only appropriate that Judge Harper make his decision on the day before Christmas."

The reporters grinned.

*   *   *

Outside, a bell began to chime. Then another one, signifying noon.

And then, without warning, a roar began to rise. Inside the judge's chambers, Harper and the others gave each other puzzled looks.

"What in the world's going on?" Alberta asked.

"Sounds like the Superbowl with the score tied and three minutes to go," said Jack Duff.

They all went to the window and stared down . . .

In disbelief.

It had started to snow. Fine white flakes drifted lazily down through the air. On the street below was a crowd that stretched away through the buildings and traffic for as far as the eye could see. And they were cheering and waving red and white banners that said, "I Believe in Santa Claus."

Cheering for Santa Claus.

Judge Harper turned from the window. He could hear the cheering ringing in his ears. He could feel the powerful gaze of Victor Lamberg burning into him. He stepped back to the desk, reached inside the valise, and took out a bundle of one-hundred-dollar bills. Still trying to make up his mind, he stared at the portrait of Benjamin Franklin on the gray side. Then he flipped the bill over to the green side and looked down at the etching of Independence Hall.

Above the etching were four words: IN GOD WE TRUST.

IN GOD . . . WE TRUST.

That man had remembered Ryan. . . .

Judge Harper remembered why he'd become a lawyer and a judge in the first place. It had something to do with justice. He slid one of the bills out of the packet. Then, with a clenched jaw and a firm sense of determination, he headed out of the room.

"Judge?" Victor Lamberg said.

Judge Harper went out without answering. A moment later he climbed up on the bench and picked up the gavel.

Bang! "This court will now come to order."

Bryan sat at the plaintiff's table and winked at Kriss, but inside, his stomach was churning. You never knew what a judge or jury would do. You simply never knew. . . .

Another door opened and Ed Collins hurried in, looking a bit pale, and took a seat at the prosecutor's desk. He gave Bryan a blank look and then looked up at the bench, where Judge Harper held up the one-hundred-dollar bill.

"This is a one-hundred-dollar bill," he told the court, which was filled with people wearing red and white buttons and carrying red and white banners. "It is issued by the treasury of the United States of America and is backed by the government and the people of the United States of America. Upon inspection of this article, or any other bill in your possession, you will see the words

IN GOD WE TRUST. While we are not here to prove that God exists, we are here to prove that a being just as invisible and yet just as present does exist. The federal government has put its trust in God. It does so on faith and faith alone. . . ."

Bryan glanced at Kriss and then at Collins. He had a feeling he knew where this was headed, but it was only a feeling.

"It is the will of the people," Judge Harper continued, "that guides the government, and it was and is their collective faith in a greater being that gave and gives cause to the inscription of this bill. If the government of the United States of America can issue its currency bearing a declaration of trust in God without demanding physical evidence of the existence or nonexistence of a greater being, the State of New York can accept and acknowledge, by similar demonstration of the collective faith of its people, that Santa Claus does exist and that he exists in the person of Kriss Kringle."

Bang! Judge Harper most emphatically and happily banged his gavel for the last time. "Case dismissed!"

From
Angels and Other Strangers

Katherine Paterson

Born in China, Katherine Paterson spent many years studying in Japan and the United States before she began writing. A two-time Newbery Medal–winning author, she has written a poignant story about angels who arrive unexpectedly and provide a glimpse into the magic of Christmas.

*M*inutes after the letter came from Arlene, Jacob set out walking for Washington. He wondered how long it would take him to get there. Before the truck died, he could make it in an hour, but he'd never tried to walk it. At sixty he knew that he didn't have the endurance that he had once had, but he was still a strong man. Perhaps he could get there by morning if he kept a steady pace. Or if he could at least reach a place where there was a bus, he could ride as far as the few bills in his pocket could take him.

Arlene needed him, so he would go to her if he had to walk every step of the way. Arlene, his baby granddaughter, whom it seemed as if he had only just stopped bouncing on his knee, was going to have a baby herself. She was alone and scared in the city and wanted her granddaddy, so he had put on his dead wife's overcoat and then his own and started out. The two coats protected him from the wet snow, but his wife's was too small and cut under his arms. "I'm coming, Arlene baby," he said to the country road. "I'm going to be with you for Christmas."

How wonderful it would be, thought Jacob, if someone stopped and offered him a ride. Occasionally a car would pass, even on this almost deserted stretch. Once he almost raised his arm to try to wave one down, but thought better of it. Who would give a ride to a black man on a lonely road? He could hope in the Lord, but he'd better rely on his own two feet. No rest, as the Good Book said, for the weary.

In Washington, Julia Thompson was humming as she worked. Why was she so happy? Because she had two beautiful children and a loving husband. Because Walter, her husband, would be singing at the Christmas Eve service, and she always felt so proud and was thrilled by his voice. Because it was nearly Christmas. Yes, of course, all those things, but, hallelujah, it was the first Christmas since she'd known Walter that she hadn't had to deal with his Aunt Patty.

Aunt Patty was Walter's only living relative. Some respect was due her for his sake, but nothing ever went quite right with Aunt Patty. The best years were the ones when she had simply grumbled her way through the celebration, taking the edge off everyone else's enjoyment. But the last three years, she'd managed to orchestrate a series of disasters, though how could you blame an old lady for falling down on the church walk just before the

Christmas Eve service and having to be rushed to the hospital with a broken hip? Perhaps Aunt Patty should have known enough not to give a two-year-old a teddy bear with button eyes which he could and would immediately pull out and swallow, but she had not known, and it had meant that they had spent Christmas Day with Kevin in the emergency room. Last year, despite Julia's apprehension, everything had gone well, until they, with great excitement, told her the news that they were expecting another child. Aunt Patty, who had never before revealed a social conscience, suddenly burst into a lament for all the starving people in the world. Here they were, gorging themselves and daring to be happy, while at the same time producing still another baby to crowd out the hungry millions.

But this year, despite Walter's urgings, Aunt Patty had decided not to make the thirty-mile trip into the city. The weather was uncertain, and her bursitis had been acting up. Julia cleaned the house and shopped and baked with an energy she hadn't possessed since before Jenny was born. She even had strength left over to take the children on long walks and read aloud to Kevin. It was going to be a wonderful Christmas.

Julia put the baby down for a nap and then took Kevin up on her own bed and began reading to him. Ordinarily, Kevin loved being read to, but today he squirmed and wriggled straight through "The Night Before Christmas."

"My, you're fidgety," she said.

"Little boys are supposed to be fidgety," he said with dignity.

She hugged him close. "Now this is the story from the Bible about when Jesus was born. Try to listen, all right?"

"All right."

She read to him the story of Mary and Joseph coming down from Nazareth to Bethlehem, stopping to explain about the taxes, the crowded inn, and the manger, going on to the shepherds in the field.

" 'And, lo, the angel of the Lord came upon them, and the glory of the Lord' — well, it's like a great light, Kevin — 'shone round about them: and they were sore afraid. And the angel said unto them, Fear not . . .' "

"Why were they afraid, Mommy?"

"I don't know — I guess the light and the strangeness. They'd never seen a real angel before."

He seemed satisfied. She read on, and since he was beginning to nod, she finished the whole chapter in a quiet voice until he was sound asleep. Julia propped pillows around him and went into the kitchen to clean up the lunch things and get ready for the evening. It was then that she discovered that they had no tangerines. Perhaps she was being silly, Kevin was only four and Jenny scarcely five months, but a Christmas stocking without a tangerine in the toe seemed somehow incomplete, and Julia was determined that this be a perfect Christmas. She got Becky the teen-ager from next door to baby-sit long enough to let her drive to the grocery store to pick up a few. She was home within twenty minutes.

"Everything quiet?" she asked the sitter.

"Sure. Fine. Your aunt called."

Julia's heart sank. "She said to tell you she'd changed her mind and would Mr. Thompson please come pick her up."

Julia should have asked Becky to stay with the children and gone then and there to get Aunt Patty, but she didn't. She paid Becky a dollar and sent her home before she tried to figure out what to do. Could she pretend she never got the message? No. She dialed Walter's office, looking at her watch as she did so. It was now three-thirty. If he could leave Washington right away, he could drive the thirty-odd miles to Bethel, pick up Aunt Patty, and get back in time for his rehearsal. But when his secretary finally answered, it was to say that there had been an accident in the plant in Virginia, and that Walter had gone out to see about it. If he called in, she would have him call home.

That settled it. It was too late. There was no way to get Aunt Patty today, unless — Reluctantly she dialed the neighbors. No, Becky had already gone out with friends. She'd tried, Julia told herself. She really had. No one would expect her to put two sleeping children in the car and drive halfway across Maryland in bad weather.

The phone rang. "Julia?" It was, of course, Aunt Patty. "I want you just to forget my message. You mustn't bother Walter about me at such a busy time. It looks like snow anyhow. It would be ridiculous to come all the way out here."

Kevin came padding down the hall in his sock feet. "Who's that, Mommy?" he asked, still half asleep.

"Aunt Patty," Julia said.

"Aunt Patty!" His face lit up. "She's coming for Christmas!"

"Now I don't want you to feel bad," Aunt Patty was saying. "Just forget all about me and have a wonderful —"

"Aunt Patty," Julia broke in wearily, "we'll be there to get you as soon as we can."

There was a silence at the other end of the line. "Well, I think it's ridiculous to try to make it out here in this weather, but. . . . Well, all right. Since you insist."

Julia woke the baby and bundled both children into the car. It was already getting dark and snowing lightly, but she couldn't honestly say that the roads were dangerous. Even driving slowly, she should have plenty of time to get out to Aunt Patty's house in the country and back in time for the service. Of course she hadn't counted on the crowded interstate on Christmas Eve afternoon. They alternately crawled and sat, motors idling, horns honking about them.

On the back seat Jenny slept while Kevin chattered away. He was so excited about getting his Aunt Patty that he sang songs about it, substituting Aunt Patty for Santa Claus. I ought to deserve some credit, Julia thought, that despite everything, I've never turned Kevin against her.

It was nearly five before they were off the main highway and moving at a decent rate of speed. If the visibility had been really poor or the road icy, Julia would have turned around for home even then. But there was no way she could escape this journey now without disappointing her little boy and making herself feel like Scrooge incarnate.

They were dangerously low on gas, but there was a station just this side of Aunt Patty's place where she could fill up, so she pushed on. When they got there, though, the station was closed for the holiday, so she drove on to Aunt Patty's house.

"Just wait with Jenny, Kevin. I'll run in and get Aunt Patty, and we'll be right back." She dashed from the driveway to the back door and banged. It was bitter cold, though the snow was slackening. She tried the door. It fell open. "Aunt Patty?" she called in the hallway. One of Aunt Patty's cats came bouncing down the steps, meowing menacingly. "Aunt Patty?" She was seized with a sudden panic that the old woman might be lying somewhere in the house, ill or worse. Then her eye fell on the note on the kitchen table.

"Walter," it said. "I've just run up to Gertrude's for a minute. You can pick me up there or wait here for me. I won't be long. Love." Walter, were he here, might know who Gertrude was, but Julia had no notion. She wouldn't even know how to look her up in the phone book.

She went back to the car.

"Where's Aunt Patty?" asked Kevin. Where indeed was Aunt Patty?

"She went to see a friend and is coming back soon. We'll go put some gas in the car. By the time we get back, she'll probably be here."

"Why'd she go away? Didn't she know we were coming?"

Julia started the engine and began backing down the drive. She was not going to ruin Christmas by losing her temper.

"Why, Mommy?"

"I don't know, Kevin. She didn't tell me."

"Did you see her?"

"No. She left a note." Addressed to Walter, naturally.

"What did the note say?"

"She just said she was going out for a few minutes and would be right back."

"Why?"

"Kevin!"

"Why'd you yell at me, Mommy?"

"Please, Kevin. I've got to watch the road." Where in the world was the nearest gas station? One that would still be open at five thirty on Christmas Eve? There was a housing development with a shopping center somewhere about — she had driven there once with Walter — if she could remember the road to take to cut over to it. Aunt Patty's road was a narrow two-lane country road with very few houses. The windshield wipers pushed the snow aside, and she sat hunched forward, peering out into the path of the headlights, not daring to glance at the gas gauge.

In the darkness, nothing looked familiar. She rarely came out here, and when she did, Walter always drove. She should have stayed and waited for Aunt Patty, but it was too late now to try to turn around and get back.

"Why are you stopping the car, Mommy?"

Julia put her head down on the wheel. She was not going to panic. She had two children to look after. She had to think clearly.

The baby woke up and began to scream.

"The baby woke up, Mommy."

"I know, sweetheart."

"Why'd you stop the car?"

"Don't get upset, Kevin. We've just run out of gas. Everything will be all right. Just don't get upset."

"I'm not upset. The baby's upset. I'm fidgety."

"Well, you can get out of your seat for a while." She reached back and undid his seat belt. He clambered happily into the front seat.

"Oh, tuna fish," he cursed, four-year-old style. "It's stopped snowing."

Julia took Jenny out of the car bed. One thing at a

time. First, the baby must be fed. As she nursed the baby, she began to sing to entertain Kevin, who was jealous that his sister could have her supper while he could not.

They were singing about glories streaming from heaven afar when Kevin spotted the light ahead. "Look, Mommy!"

Jacob had first seen the headlights come quickly over a rise far down the road and then as quickly disappear. He kept walking, swinging his huge flashlight as he went, expecting them to reappear at any moment. Not that it mattered. The car was heading the wrong way for him anyhow, even if by some miracle it was someone who would consider giving him a ride. At least it had stopped snowing. Just then the beam of his flashlight caught a car sitting in the darkness. There were people inside. He hesitated a moment. What if it were a trick? For himself he didn't mind dying. Lord knew he was ready to go, but Arlene needed him now. He had to get to Washington. Yet here, perhaps, was somebody else in need. He started across the road, heading for the driver's side of the car.

"Look, Mommy!" Kevin said again. "Glory streams from heaven afar." A strong bright light moved over the rise and down the hill toward them. Julia stopped singing and watched it come. Finally, behind the light, she could make out the tall bulging shadow of a man. She checked quickly to make sure all the doors were locked, took the baby off her breast, and straightened her clothes with a shaking hand. The light was coming straight for her window. Her eyes blinked to shut out the brightness, and when she opened them, a huge black face, which seemed to fill the side window of the small car, was there within inches of her cheek. She pulled back. The man tapped on the window with a worn brown glove that showed the tips of his fingers, and said something through the glass. Julia squeezed the baby tighter and stared straight ahead.

Kevin leaned across her and banged the glass. "Hi!" he said.

"Hi yourself."

Out of the corner of her eye Julia could see the black face smiling broadly. The chin was covered with silver bristles and several teeth were missing. She tried to grab Kevin to shush him.

"Need some help?" This time the man was shouting as though to make sure she could hear him plainly through the window, but she refused to turn her head.

"Mommy, why don't you answer the nice man?"

"Shh, Kevin. We don't know what he wants."

"He wants to know if we need some help."

The man leaned close to the glass and shouted again. "Don't be afraid, little lady."

"You hear that, Mommy?"

"Kevin, please."

"But, Mommy, he said, 'Don't be afraid!' That's what *angels* say."

"Kevin, no!"

But before she could catch him, Kevin had slid across the seat, pulled up the button, opened the door, and jumped out of the car. The man immediately started around to meet him.

"Don't you touch my child!" Julia screamed, twisting awkwardly from under the wheel, still clutching the baby.

"You don't want him running out into the road, do you, lady?"

"No. No. Thank you." She took Kevin's hand.

"I saw your car and figured you was in trouble."

There was no way to ignore him now. But she had to be careful. He was over six feet tall and obviously strong. The police-pamphlet directions flashed across her brain: *Be sure to look carefully at your assailant so you can give an accurate description to the police later.* If there was a later. Oh, God, don't let him hurt me. Don't let him hurt the children.

"We ran out of gas," said Kevin.

Why was she so afraid of him? He, Jacob, who had never willfully hurt the least one of God's creatures — couldn't she tell by looking at him that he only wanted to help? Even the child could see that. He stretched out his hand to put it on the boy's head, but seeing the look in the woman's eyes, he brought it back.

"Your old car's got an empty belly, huh?"

The boy giggled. "Me, too," he said. "I haven't even had my supper."

"Well, we gotta do something about that. I passed a gas station a while back," Jacob said to the woman. "You don't have a can, do you?"

She shook her head. She seemed to be shivering.

"You better get back in the car and try to stay warm." He turned and started back up the hill, sighing as he retraced the descent of a few minutes before. It seemed to have grown steeper. But, at least, praise the Lord, the snow had stopped and the sky was clearing.

"Wait," she called after him. "You'll need some money."

"I got some," Jacob said. He didn't want to waste time and energy going back down the hill.

Suppose he never came back? Would they grow cold and sleepy and freeze out here in the middle of nowhere on Christmas Eve? Well, Aunt Patty, you will have certainly beaten your own record this year — even Christmas morning in the emergency room will pale in comparison. And then suppose he did come back? What did he want? He could have just taken her purse and run, if money was what he wanted. But of course it was the car he was after, so he could get away faster — but she tried not to think of that.

"I think we should sing some more songs," Kevin said. "I might forget about my tummy."

Julia was glad for the diversion. They sang through every carol she knew, even la-la-ing through unfamiliar verses. Then they sang all the songs on Kevin's favorite records, then another round of Christmas carols. Until at long last they saw the light coming over the hill.

"Here comes the glory light," said Kevin.

This time when the man came to her window, she rolled it down. "Would you hold the flashlight for me while I pour the gas in?" he asked.

Trembling, she laid Jenny down in the car bed and went around to the tank. He handed her his big torch, which she tried to hold steady as he poured.

"Well, thank you," Julia said when he had finished, keeping her voice cool. "Let me pay you something for all your trouble."

Jacob looked at her. She was going to give him some money and drive off. He had given her nearly an hour of his time and far more of his energy than he could spare. There was no way she could pay him for that. But she had already gone to the front seat and gotten her purse, the little boy scampering around her at every step.

"That's all right," he said. "Forget it."

She stuck a few bills out at him. "But I owe you for the gas."

"I — uh — do need to return the can. If you could give me a ride down the road and back. . . ."

She nodded.

He could tell by her eyes that she didn't want him in her car, but, Lord, she owed him that much. He decided to ignore her eyes.

"Well, old man," he said to the child, "let's see if we can get this old buggy going." He took the boy around and put him in his seat, letting the child tell him how to buckle the belt, and then climbed into the front seat.

The woman put her purse down between them and buckled herself in. Jacob looked down at the purse and then realized she had caught him looking. He quickly shifted his gaze. "Just down the road a couple of miles or so," he said.

Within ten minutes they were at the lighted station. She gave the can back to the attendant and asked him to fill the tank. She saw his eyes question the presence of the man on the seat beside her. Should she try to signal for help? It seemed too foolish. The man had done nothing except try to help her — so far. She at least owed him a ride home on this freezing night.

"We come to get my Aunt Patty to take her home for Christmas." Oh, Kevin.

"Is that a fact? Where's your home, old man?"

Don't answer him, Kevin. But of course Kevin, who had memorized his full address at nursery school, recited it in a proud singsong: "Thirteen-oh-six Essex Street Northwest, Washington, D.C. Two-oh-oh-one-six."

"My, you're one smart boy."

"I know," said Kevin.

I could get a ride all the way to Washington tonight, Jacob said to himself. All I have to do is ask. But he couldn't make himself say the words. If the woman had seemed in the least bit friendly, the least bit trusting, he would have asked her. But how could he ask a favor of a person who thought he was going to grab her purse or hurt her kids?

She had started the car and was pulling out of the station. "Where shall I let you off?" she asked.

It was his chance to tell her. She owed him something, didn't she? And Arlene was waiting, not even knowing if he had gotten her letter.

"Just down the road," he mumbled. "Just anywhere."

They drove past the place where they had met, but he gave no sign of wanting to be let out, so Julia drove on. She couldn't just stop in the middle of nowhere and order him out. What should she do? They went on until she could see Aunt Patty's house ablaze with light. Aunt Patty was home. Thank God for small blessings.

"Here's where my Aunt Patty lives," Kevin told the stranger.

"Is that a fact?"

The problem of how to get Aunt Patty without leaving the children alone in the car with the man solved itself. Aunt Patty came rushing out of the house, coat and suitcases flying. She had obviously been watching for the car. When she saw Julia at the wheel, she was furious. "Where have you been?" she demanded. "You're going to make me miss the music."

Julia opened her mouth to defend herself, but at the same moment her passenger got out of the car. He stood there tall and straight against the starry winter sky.

"Mercy!" Aunt Patty screamed. "What in the world?"

"He's our angel, Aunt Patty. Our Christmas angel."

"Don't be ridiculous, Kevin."

Ridiculous indeed! All Julia's fears evaporated in a puff of anger. How dare Aunt Patty call it ridiculous? The man had been an angel. She leaned across the seat and called out, "Would you mind squeezing in back with the children?"

Even in the darkness she thought she could see him smile.

"Get in, Aunt Patty," she commanded, "or you'll make us miss the music."

A little farther down the road she turned to him. "How far can I take you?"

"I need to go all the way to Washington," he said.

"Oh, goody!" cried Kevin. "Then you can go to church with us! We never had a real angel in our church before."

73

He patted the boy's knee. "Can't make it this time, old man," he said. "I got to go see this lonesome little girl. Cheer her up for Christmas."

"Angels are really busy, aren't they?"

Jacob laughed, a great rich sound which filled the car. "Yeah," he said. "We keep busy, but it's mighty pleasant work."

Aunt Patty may have said something that sounded like "ridiculous," but Julia joyfully chose to ignore it. This was going to be a perfect Christmas.

The Gift of the Magi

O. Henry

O. Henry was the pen name of William Sidney Porter, considered by many to be among the greatest American storytellers. His simple short stories were noted for their ironic coincidences and their surprise endings. First published in a collection in 1906, this story showcases the sacrifices of lovers and the endurance of the Christmas spirit.

One dollar and eighty-seven cents. That was all. And sixty cents of it was in pennies. Pennies saved one and two at a time by bulldozing the grocer and the vegetable man and the butcher until one's cheeks burned with the silent imputation of parsimony that such close dealing implied. Three times Della counted it. One dollar and eighty-seven cents. And the next day would be Christmas.

There was clearly nothing to do but flop down on the shabby little couch and howl. So Della did it. Which instigates the moral reflection that life is made up of sobs, sniffles, and smiles, with sniffles predominating.

While the mistress of the home is gradually subsiding from the first stage to the second, take a look at the home. A furnished flat at eight dollars per week. It did not exactly beggar description, but it certainly had that word on the lookout for the mendicancy squad.

In the vestibule below was a letter-box into which no letter would go, and an electric button from which no mortal finger could coax a ring. Also appertaining thereunto was a card bearing the name "Mr. James Dillingham Young."

The "Dillingham" had been flung to the breeze during a former period of prosperity when its possessor was being paid thirty dollars per week. Now, when the income was shrunk to twenty dollars, the letters of "Dillingham" looked blurred, as though they were thinking seriously of contracting to a modest and unassuming D. But whenever Mr. James Dillingham Young came home and reached his flat above he was called "Jim" and greatly hugged by Mrs. James Dillingham Young, already introduced to you as Della. Which is all very good.

Della finished her cry and attended to her cheeks with a powder puff. She stood by the window and looked out dully at a gray cat walking a gray fence in a gray back yard. Tomorrow would be Christmas Day, and she had only $1.87 with which to buy Jim a present. She had been saving every penny she could for months, with this result. Twenty dollars a week doesn't go far. Expenses had been greater than she had calculated. They always are. Only $1.87 to buy a present for Jim. Her Jim. Many a happy hour she had spent planning for something nice for him. Something fine and rare and sterling — something just a little bit near to being worthy of the honor of being owned by Jim.

There was a pier-glass between the windows of the room. Perhaps you have seen a pier-glass in an eight-dollar flat. A very thin and very agile person may, by observing his reflection in a rapid sequence of longitudinal strips, obtain a fairly accurate conception of his looks. Della, being slender, had mastered the art.

Suddenly she whirled from the window and stood before the glass. Her eyes were shining brilliantly, but her face had lost its color within twenty seconds. Rapidly she pulled down her hair and let it fall to its full length.

Now, there were two possessions of the James Dillingham Youngs in which they both took a mighty pride. One was Jim's gold watch that had been his father's and his grandfather's. The other was Della's hair. Had the Queen of Sheba lived in the flat across the airshaft, Della would have let her hair hang out the window some day to dry just to depreciate Her Majesty's jewels and gifts. Had King Solomon been the janitor, with all his treasures piled up in the basement, Jim would have pulled out his watch every day he passed, just to see him pluck at his beard from envy.

So now Della's beautiful hair fell about her, rippling and shining like a cascade of brown waters. She did it up again nervously and quickly. Once she faltered for a minute and stood still while a tear or two splashed on the worn red carpet.

On went her old brown jacket, on went her old brown hat. With a whirl of skirts and with the brilliant sparkle still in her eyes, she fluttered out the door and down the stairs to the street.

Where she stopped the sign read: "Mme. Sofronie.

Hair Goods of All Kinds." One flight up Della ran, and collected herself, panting. Madame, large, too white, chilly, hardly looked the "Sofronie."

"Will you buy my hair?" asked Della.

"I buy hair," said Madame. "Take yer hat off and let's have a sight at the looks of it."

Down rippled the brown cascade.

"Twenty dollars," said Madame, lifting the mass with a practiced hand.

"Give it to me quick," said Della.

Oh, and the next two hours tripped by on rosy wings. Forget the hashed metaphor. She was ransacking the stores for Jim's present.

She found it at last. It surely had been made for Jim and no one else. There was no other like it in any of the stores, and she had turned all of them inside out. It was a platinum watch-chain, simple and chaste in design, properly proclaiming its value by substance alone and not by meretricious ornamentation — as all good things should do. It was even worthy of The Watch. As soon as she saw it she knew that it must be Jim's. It was like him. Quietness and value — the description applied to both. Twenty-one dollars they took from her for it, and she hurried home with the eighty-seven cents. With that chain on his watch Jim might be properly anxious about the time in any company. Grand as the watch was, he sometimes looked at it on the sly on account of the old leather strap that he used in place of a chain.

When Della reached home her intoxication gave way a little to prudence and reason. She got out her curling-irons and lighted the gas and went to work repairing the ravages made by generosity added to love. Which is always a tremendous task, dear friends — a mammoth task.

Within forty minutes her head was covered with tiny close-lying curls that made her look wonderfully like a truant schoolboy. She looked at her reflection in the mirror long, carefully, and critically.

"If Jim doesn't kill me," she said to herself, "before he takes a second look at me, he'll say I look like a Coney Island chorus girl. But what could I do — Oh! what could I do with a dollar and eighty-seven cents?"

At seven o'clock the coffee was made and the frying-pan was on the back of the stove, hot and ready to cook the chops.

Jim was never late. Della doubled the watch-chain in her hand and sat on the corner of the table near the door that he always entered. Then she heard his step in the stair way down on the first flight, and she turned white for just a moment. She had a habit of saying little silent prayers about the simplest everyday things, and now she whispered, "Please God, make him think I am still pretty."

The door opened and Jim stepped in and closed it. He looked thin and very serious. Poor fellow, he was only twenty-two — and to be burdened with a family! He needed a new overcoat and he was without gloves.

Jim stepped inside the door, as immovable as a setter at the scent of quail. His eyes were fixed upon Della, and there was an expression in them that she could not read, and it terrified her. It was not anger, nor surprise, nor disapproval, nor horror, nor any of the sentiments that she had been prepared for. He simply stared at her fixedly with that peculiar expression on his face.

Della wriggled off the table and went for him.

"Jim, darling," she cried, "don't look at me that way. I had my hair cut off and sold it because I couldn't have lived through Christmas without giving you a present. It'll grow out again — you won't mind, will you? I just had to do it. My hair grows awfully fast. Say 'Merry Christmas!' Jim, and let's be happy. You don't know what a nice — what a beautiful, nice gift I've got for you."

"You've cut off your hair?" asked Jim, laboriously, as if he had not arrived at that patent fact yet even after the hardest mental labor.

"Cut it off and sold it," said Della. "Don't you like me just as well, anyhow? I'm me without my hair, ain't I?"

Jim looked about the room curiously.

"You say your hair is gone?" he said, with an air almost of idiocy.

"You needn't look for it," said Della. "It's sold, I tell you — sold and gone, too. It's Christmas Eve, boy. Be good to me, for it went for you. Maybe the hairs of my head were numbered," she went on with a sudden serious sweetness, "but nobody could ever count my love for you. Shall I put the chops on, Jim?"

Out of his trance Jim seemed to quickly wake. He enfolded his Della. For ten seconds let us regard with discreet scrutiny some inconsequential object in the other direction. Eight dollars a week or a million a year — what is the difference? A mathematician or a wit would give you the wrong answer. The Magi brought valuable gifts, but that was not among them. This dark assertion will be illuminated later on.

Jim drew a package from his overcoat pocket and threw it upon the table.

"Don't make any mistake, Dell," he said, "about me. I don't think there's anything in the way of a haircut or a shave or a shampoo that could make me like my girl any less. But if you'll unwrap that package you may see why you had me going awhile at first."

White fingers and nimble tore at the string and paper. And then an ecstatic scream of joy; and then, alas! a quick feminine change to hysterical tears and wails, necessitating the immediate employment of all the comforting powers of the lord of the flat.

For there lay The Combs — the set of combs that Della had worshiped for long in a Broadway window. Beautiful combs, pure tortoise shell, with jeweled rims — just the shade to wear in the beautiful vanished hair. They were expensive combs, she knew, and her heart had simply craved and yearned over them without the least hope of possession. And now they were hers, but the tresses that should have adorned the coveted adornments were gone.

But she hugged them to her bosom, and at length she was able to look up with dim eyes and a smile and say: "My hair grows so fast, Jim!"

And then Della leaped up like a little singed cat and cried, "Oh, oh!"

Jim had not yet seen his beautiful present. She held it out to him eagerly upon her open palm. The dull precious metal seemed to flash with a reflection of her bright and ardent spirit.

"Isn't it a dandy, Jim? I hunted all over town to find it. You'll have to look at the time a hundred times a day now. Give me your watch. I want to see how it looks on it."

Instead of obeying, Jim tumbled down on the couch and put his hands under the back of his head and smiled.

"Dell," he said, "let's put our Christmas presents away and keep 'em awhile. They're too nice to use just at present. I sold the watch to get the money to buy your combs. And now suppose you put the chops on."

The Magi, as you know, were wise men — wonderfully wise men — who brought gifts to the Babe in the manger. They invented the art of giving Christmas presents. Being wise, their gifts were no doubt wise ones, possibly bearing the privilege of exchange in case of duplication. And here I have lamely related to you the uneventful chronicle of two foolish children in a flat who most unwisely sacrificed for each other the greatest treasures of their house. But in a last word to the wise of these days let it be said that of all who give gifts these two were the wisest. Of all who give and receive gifts, such as they are wisest. Everywhere they are wisest. They are the Magi.

The Fir-Tree

Hans Christian Andersen

Hans Christian Andersen, recognized as one of the masters of the fairy-tale genre, was born in Denmark in 1805 to a poor shoemaker and his wife. Andersen's childhood was not a happy one, but he followed his dreams and fought his way up from poverty to become one of the most famous and best-loved authors of all time.

*O*ut in the woods stood a nice little Fir-tree. The place he had was a very good one; the sun shone on him; as to fresh air, there was enough of that, and round him grew many large-sized comrades, pines as well as firs. But the little Fir wanted so very much to be a grown-up tree.

He did not think of the warm sun and of the fresh air; he did not care for the little cottage-children that ran about and prattled when they were in the woods looking for wild strawberries. The children often came with a whole pitcher full of berries, or a long row of them threaded on a straw, and sat down near the young Tree and said, "O, how pretty he is! What a nice little fir!" But this was what the Tree could not bear to hear.

At the end of a year he had shot up a good deal, and after another year, he was another long bit taller; for with fir-trees one can always tell by the shoots how many years old they are.

"O, were I but such a high tree as the others are," sighed he. "Then I should be able to spread out my branches, and with the tops to look into the wide world! Then would the birds build nests among my branches; and when there was a breeze, I could bend with as much stateliness as the others!"

Neither the sunbeams, nor the birds, nor the red clouds which morning and evening sailed above him, gave the little Tree any pleasure.

In winter, when the snow lay glittering on the ground, a hare would often come leaping along, and jump right over the little Tree. Oh, that made him so angry! But two winters were past, and in the third the Tree was so large that the hare was obliged to go round it. "To grow and grow, to get older and be tall," thought the Tree; "that, after all, is the most delightful thing in the world!"

In autumn, the wood-cutters always came and felled some of the largest trees. This happened every year; and the young Fir-tree, that had now grown to a very comely size, trembled at the sight; for the magnificent great trees fell to the earth with noise and crackling, the branches were lopped off, and the trees looked long and bare: they were hardly to be recognized; and then they were laid in carts, and the horses dragged them out of the wood.

Where did they go? What became of them?

In spring, when the Swallows and the Storks came, the Tree asked them, "Don't you know where they have been taken? Have you not met them anywhere?"

The Swallows did not know anything about it; but the Stork looked, musing, nodded his head, and said, "Yes; I think I know; I met many ships as I was flying hither from Egypt; on the ships were magnificent masts, and I venture to assert that it was they that smelt so of fir. I may congratulate you, for they lifted themselves on high most majestically!"

"O, were I but old enough to fly across the sea! But how does the sea look in reality? What is it like?"

"That would take a long time to explain," said the Stork, and with these words off he went.

"Rejoice in thy growth!" said the Sunbeams; "rejoice in thy vigorous growth, and in the fresh life that moveth within thee!"

And the Wind kissed the Tree, and the Dew wept tears over him; but the Fir understood it not.

When Christmas came, quite young trees were cut down; trees which often were not even as large or of the same age as this Fir-tree, who could never rest, but always wanted to be off. These young trees, and they were always the finest looking, retained their branches; they were laid on carts, and the horses drew them out of the wood.

"Where are they going to?" asked the Fir. "They are no taller than I —" there was one indeed that was considerably shorter —"and why do they retain all their branches? Whither are they taken?"

"We know! we know!" chirped the Sparrows. "We have peeped in at the windows in the town below! We know whither they are taken! The greatest splendor and the

91

greatest magnificence one can imagine await them. We peeped through the windows, and saw them planted in the middle of the warm room, and ornamented with the most splendid things — with gilded apples, with ginger-bread, with toys, and many hundred lights!"

"And then?" asked the Fir-tree, trembling in every bough. "And then? What happens then?"

"We did not see anything more: it was incomparably beautiful."

"I would fain know if I am destined for so glorious a career," cried the Tree, rejoicing. "That is still better than to cross the sea! What a longing do I suffer! Were Christmas but come! I am now tall, and my branches spread like the others that were carried off last year! O, were I but already on the cart! Were I in the warm room with all the splendor and magnificence! Yes; then something better, something still grander, will surely follow, or wherefore should they thus ornament me? Something better, something still grander, *must* follow — but what? O, how I long, how I suffer! I do not know myself what is the matter with me!"

"Rejoice in our presence!" said the Air and the Sunlight; "rejoice in thy own fresh youth!"

But the Tree did not rejoice at all; he grew and grew, and was green both winter and summer. People who saw him said, "What a fine tree!" and towards Christmas he was one of the first that was cut down. The axe stuck deep into the very pith; the Tree fell to the earth with a sigh: he felt a pang — it was like a swoon; he could not think of happiness, for he was sorrowful at being separated from his home, from the place where he had sprung up. He well knew that he should never see his dear old comrades, the little bushes and flowers around him, any more; perhaps not even the birds! The departure was not at all agreeable.

The Tree only came to himself when he was unloaded in a court-yard with the other trees, and heard a man say, "That one is splendid! we don't want the others." Then two servants came in rich livery and carried the Fir-tree into a large and splendid drawing-room. Portraits were hanging on the walls, and near the white porcelain stove stood two large Chinese vases with lions on the covers. There, too, were large easy-chairs, silken sofas, large tables full of picture-books, and full of toys worth hundreds and hundreds of crowns — at least the children said so. And the Fir-tree was stuck upright in a cask that was filled with sand: but no one could see that it was a cask, for green cloth was hung all round it, and it stood on a large gayly-colored carpet. O, how the tree quivered! What was to happen? The servants, as well as the young ladies, decorated it. On one branch there were hung little nets cut out of colored paper, and each net was filled with sugar-plums; and among the other boughs gilded apples and walnuts were suspended, looking as though they had grown there, and little blue and white tapers were placed among the

leaves. Dolls that looked for all the world like men —
the Tree had never beheld such before — were seen
among the foliage, and at the very top a large star of gold
tinsel was fixed. It was really splendid — beyond description splendid.

"This evening!" said they all; "how it will shine this
evening!"

"O," thought the Tree, "if the evening were but come!
If the tapers were but lighted! And then I wonder what
will happen! Perhaps the other trees from the forest will
come to look at me! Perhaps the sparrows will beat
against the window-panes! I wonder if I shall take root
here, and winter and summer stand covered with ornaments!"

He knew very much about the matter! But he was so
impatient that for sheer longing he got a pain in his
back, and this with trees is the same thing as a head-
ache with us.

The candles were now lighted. What brightness!
What splendor! The Tree trembled so in every bough
that one of the tapers set fire to the foliage. It blazed up
splendidly.

"Help! help!" cried the young ladies, and they quickly
put out the fire.

Now the Tree did not even dare tremble. What a state
he was in! He was so uneasy lest he should lose something of his splendor, that he was quite bewildered
amidst the glare and brightness; when suddenly both

folding-doors opened, and a troop of children rushed in as if they would upset the Tree. The older persons followed quietly; the little ones stood quite still. But it was only for a moment; then they shouted so that the whole place re-echoed with their rejoicing; they danced round the Tree, and one present after the other was pulled off.

"What are they about?" thought the Tree. "What is to happen now!" And the lights burned down to the very branches, and as they burned down they were put out one after the other, and then the children had permission to plunder the Tree. So they fell upon it with such violence that all its branches cracked; if it had not been fixed firmly in the cask, it would certainly have tumbled down.

The children danced about with their beautiful playthings: no one looked at the Tree except the old nurse, who peeped between the branches; but it was only to see if there was a fig or an apple left that had been forgotten.

"A story! a story!" cried the children, drawing a little fat man towards the Tree. He seated himself under it, and said, "Now we are in the shade, and the Tree can listen too. But I shall tell only one story. Now which will you have; about Ivedy-Avedy, or about Klumpy-Dumpy who tumbled downstairs, and yet after all came to the throne and married the princess?"

"Ivedy-Avedy," cried some; "Klumpy-Dumpy," cried the others. There was such a bawling and screaming! — the Fir-tree alone was silent, and he thought to himself, "Am I not to bawl with the rest? — am I to do nothing whatever?" for he was one of the company, and had done what he had to do.

And the man told about Klumpy-Dumpy who tumbled down, who notwithstanding came to the throne, and at last married the princess. And the children clapped their hands, and cried out, "O, go on! Do go on!" They wanted to hear about Ivedy-Avedy too, but the little man only told them about Klumpy-Dumpy. The Fir-tree stood quite still and absorbed in thought: the birds in the wood had never related the like of this. "Klumpy-Dumpy fell downstairs, and yet he married the princess! Yes, yes! that's the way of the world!" thought the Fir-tree, and believed it all, because the man who told the story was so good-looking. "Well, well! who knows, perhaps I may fall downstairs too, and get a princess as wife!" And he looked forward with joy to the morrow, when he hoped to be decked out again with lights, playthings, fruits, and tinsel.

"I won't tremble to-morrow!" thought the Fir-tree. "I will enjoy to the full all my splendor! To-morrow I shall hear again the story of Klumpy-Dumpy, and perhaps that of Ivedy-Avedy too." And the whole night the Tree stood still in deep thought.

In the morning the servant and the housemaid came in.

"Now then the splendor will begin again," thought the Fir. But they dragged him out of the room, and up the stairs into the loft; and here in a dark corner, where no daylight could enter, they left him. "What's the meaning of this?" thought the Tree. "What am I to do here? What shall I hear now, I wonder?" And he leaned against the wall lost in reverie. Time enough had he too for his reflections; for days and nights passed on, and nobody came up; and when at last somebody did come, it was only to put some great trunks in a corner out of the way. There stood the Tree quite hidden; it seemed as if he had been entirely forgotten.

" 'Tis now winter out-of-doors!" thought the Tree. "The earth is hard and covered with snow; men cannot plant me now, and therefore I have been put up here under shelter till the spring-time comes! How thoughtful that is! How kind man is, after all! If it only were not so dark here, and so terribly lonely! Not even a hare. And out in the woods it was so pleasant, when the snow was on the ground and the hare leaped by; yes — even when he jumped over me; but I did not like it then. It is really terribly lonely here!"

"Squeak! squeak!" said a little Mouse at the same moment, peeping out of his hole. And then another little one came. They snuffed about the Fir-tree, and rustled among the branches.

"It is dreadfully cold," said the Mouse. "But for that, it would be delightful here, old Fir, wouldn't it?"

"I am by no means old," said the Fir-tree. "There's many a one considerably older than I am."

"Where do you come from," asked the Mice; "and what can you do?" They were so extremely curious. "Tell us about the most beautiful spot on the earth. Have you never been there? Were you never in the larder, where cheeses lie on the shelves, and hams hang from above; where one dances about on tallow candles; that place where one enters lean, and comes out again fat and portly?"

"I know no such place," said the Tree. "But I know the wood, where the sun shines, and where the little birds sing." And then he told all about his youth; and the little Mice had never heard the like before, and they listened and said,

"Well, to be sure! How much you have seen! How happy you must have been!"

"I!" said the Fir-tree, thinking over what he had himself related. "Yes, in reality those were happy times." And then he told about Christmas Eve, when he was decked out with cakes and candles.

"O," said the little Mice, "how fortunate you have been, old Fir-tree!"

"I am by no means old," said he. "I came from the wood this winter; I am in my prime, and am only rather short for my age."

"What delightful stories you know!" said the Mice: and the next night they came with four other little Mice, who were to hear what the Tree recounted; and the more he related, the more plainly he remembered all himself; and it appeared as if those times had really been happy times. "But they may still come — they may still come. Klumpy-Dumpy fell downstairs, and yet he got a princess!" and he thought at the moment of a nice little Birch-tree growing out in the woods: to the Fir, that would be a real charming princess.

"Who is Klumpy-Dumpy?" asked the Mice. So then the Fir-tree told the whole fairy tale, for he could remember every single word of it; and the little Mice jumped for joy up to the very top of the Tree. Next night two more Mice came, and on Sunday two Rats, even; but they said the stories were not interesting, which vexed the little Mice; and they, too, now began to think them not so very amusing either.

"Do you know only one story?" asked the Rats.

"Only that one," answered the Tree. "I heard it on my happiest evening, but I did not then know how happy I was."

"It is a very stupid story! Don't you know one about bacon and tallow candles? Can't you tell any larder-stories?"

"No," said the Tree.

"Then good-by," said the Rats; and they went home.

At last the little Mice stayed away also; and the Tree sighed: "After all, it was very pleasant when the sleek little Mice sat round me and listened to what I told them. Now that too is over. But I will take good care to enjoy myself when I am brought out again."

But when was that to be? Why, one morning there came a quantity of people and they set to work in the loft. The trunks were moved, the tree was pulled out and thrown — rather hard, it is true — down on the floor, but a man drew him towards the stairs, where the daylight shone.

"Now a merry life will begin again," thought the Tree. He felt the fresh air, the first sunbeam, and now he was out in the court-yard. All passed so quickly, there was so much going on around him, that the Tree quite forgot to look to himself. The court adjoined a garden, and all was in flower; the roses hung so fresh and odorous over the balustrade, the lindens were in blossom, the Swallows flew by, and said, "Quirre-vit! my husband is come!" but it was not the Fir-tree that they meant.

"Now, then, I shall really enjoy life," said he, exultingly, and spread out his branches; but, alas! they were all withered and yellow. It was in a corner that he lay, among weeds and nettles. The golden star of tinsel was still on the top of the Tree, and glittered in the sunshine.

In the court-yard some of the merry children were playing who had danced at Christmas round the Fir-tree, and were so glad at the sight of him. One of the youngest ran and tore off the golden star.

"Only look what is still on the ugly old Christmas tree!" said he, trampling on the branches, so that they all cracked beneath his feet.

And the Tree beheld all the beauty of the flowers, and

the freshness in the garden; he beheld himself, and wished he had remained in his dark corner in the loft: he thought of his first youth in the wood, of the merry Christmas Eve, and of the little Mice, who had listened with so much pleasure to the story of Klumpy-Dumpy.

"'Tis over — 'tis past!" said the poor Tree. "Had I but rejoiced when I had reason to do so! But now 'tis past, 'tis past!"

And the gardener's boy chopped the Tree into small pieces; there was a whole heap lying there. The wood flamed up splendidly under the large brewing copper, and it sighed so deeply! Each sigh was like a shot.

The boys played about in the court, and the youngest wore the gold star on his breast, which the Tree had had on the happiest evening of his life. However, that was over now — the Tree gone, the story at an end. All, all was over; every tale must end at last.

From
The Best Christmas Pageant Ever

Barbara Robinson

It's time for the annual Christmas pageant, but Mrs. Armstrong, who usually runs the show, is in the hospital with a broken leg. And that's not the only thing to go wrong. The Herdman kids — who have never been to Sunday school and are known as the school bullies — are cast in all the main parts. Still, the actual pageant is full of surprises for everyone, starting with the Herdmans themselves.

$\mathcal{M}$rs. Armstrong, who was still trying to run things from her hospital bed, said that the same people always got the main parts. "But it's important to give everybody a chance," she told Mother over the telephone. "Let me tell you what I do."

Mother sighed, and turned off the heat under the pork chops. "All right, Helen," she said.

Mrs. Armstrong called Mother at least every other day, and she always called at suppertime. "Don't let me interrupt your supper," she always said, and then went right ahead and did it anyway, while my father paced up and down the hall, saying things under his breath about Mrs. Armstrong.

"Here's what I do," Mrs. Armstrong said. "I get them all together and tell them about the rehearsals, and that they must be on time and pay close attention. Then I tell them that the main parts are Mary and Joseph and the Wise Men and the Angel of the Lord. And then I always remind them that there are no small parts, only small actors."

"Do they understand what that means?" Mother asked.

"Oh, yes," Mrs. Armstrong said.

Later Mother asked me if I knew what that meant, about small parts and small actors.

I didn't really know — none of us did. It was just something Mrs. Armstrong always said. "I guess it means that the short kids have to be in the front row of the angel choir, or else nobody can see them."

"I thought so," Mother said. "It doesn't mean that at all. It really means that every single person in the pageant is just as important as every other person — that the littlest baby angel is just as important as Mary."

"Go and tell that to Alice Wendleken," I said, and Mother told me not to be so fresh. She didn't get very mad, though, because she knew I was right. You could have a Christmas pageant without *any* baby angels, but you couldn't have one without a Mary.

Mrs. Armstrong knew it too. "I always start with Mary," she told Mother over the telephone. "I tell them that we must choose our Mary carefully, because Mary was the mother of Jesus."

"I know that," Mother said, wanting to get off the telephone and cook the pork chops.

"Yes. I tell them that our Mary should be a cheerful, happy little girl who is unselfish and kind to others. Then I tell them about Joseph, that he was God's choice to be Jesus' father, and our Joseph ought to be a little boy . . . "
She went on and on and got as far as the second Wise

Man when Mother said, "Helen, I'll have to go now. There's somebody at the door."

Actually there was somebody at the door. It was my father, standing out on the porch in his coat and hat, leaning on the doorbell.

When Mother let him in he took off his hat and bowed to her. "Lady, can you give me some supper? I haven't had a square meal in three days."

"Oh, for goodness' sake," Mother said, "come on in. What will the neighbors think, to see you standing out there ringing your own doorbell? And why didn't you ring the doorbell ten minutes ago?"

Mrs. Armstrong called Mother two more times that week — to tell her that people could hem up costumes, but couldn't cut them — and to tell her not to let the angel choir wear lipstick. And by Sunday, Mother was already sick of the whole thing.

After church we all filed into the back seven pews, along with two or three Sunday-school teachers who were supposed to keep everybody quiet. It was a terrible time to try to keep everybody quiet — all the little kids were tired and all the big kids were hungry, and all the mothers wanted to go home and cook dinner, and all the fathers wanted to go home and watch the football game on TV.

"Now, this isn't going to take very long," Mother told us. My father had said it better not take very long, because he wanted to watch the football game too. He also wanted to eat, he said — he hadn't had a decent meal all week.

"First I'm going to tell you about the rehearsals," Mother said. "We'll have our rehearsals on Wednesdays at 6:30. We're only going to have five rehearsals so you must all try to be present at every one."

"What if we get sick?" asked a little kid in the front pew.

"You won't get sick," Mother told him, which was exactly what she told Charlie that morning when Charlie said he didn't want to be a shepherd and would be sick to his stomach if she made him be one.

"Now you little children in the cradle room and the primary class will be our angels," Mother said. "You'll like that, won't you?"

They all said yes. What else could they say?

"The older boys and girls will be shepherds and guests at the inn and members of the choir." Mother was really zipping along, and I thought how mad Mrs. Armstrong would be about all the things she was leaving out.

"And we need Mary and Joseph, the three Wise Men, and the Angel of the Lord. They aren't hard parts, but they're very important parts, so those people must absolutely come to every rehearsal."

"What if *they* get sick?" It was the same little kid, and it made you wonder what kind of little kid he was, to be so interested in sickness.

"They won't get sick either," Mother said, looking a

little cross. "Now, we all know what kind of person Mary was. She was quiet and gentle and kind, and the little girl who plays Mary should try to be that kind of person. I know that many of you would like to be Mary in our pageant, but of course we can only have one Mary. So I'll ask for volunteers, and then we'll all decide together which girl should get the part." That was pretty safe to say, since the only person who ever raised her hand was Alice Wendleken.

But Alice just sat there, chewing on a piece of her hair and looking down at the floor . . . and the only person who raised her hand this time was Imogene Herdman.

"Did you have a question, Imogene?" Mother asked. I guess that was the only reason she could think of for Imogene to have her hand up.

"No," Imogene said. "I want to be Mary." She looked back over her shoulder. "And Ralph wants to be Joseph."

"Yeh," Ralph said.

Mother just stared at them. It was like a detective movie, when the nice little old gray-haired lady sticks a gun in the bank window and says "Give me all your money" and you can't believe it. Mother couldn't believe this.

"Well," she said after a minute, "we want to be sure that everyone has a chance. Does anyone else want to volunteer for Joseph?"

No one did. No one ever did, especially not Elmer

Hopkins. But he couldn't do anything about it, because he was the minister's son. One year he didn't volunteer to be Joseph and neither did anyone else, and afterward I heard Reverend Hopkins talking to Elmer out in the hall.

"You're going to be Joseph," Reverend Hopkins said. "That's it."

"I don't want to be Joseph," Elmer told him. "I'm too big, and I feel dumb up there, and all those little kids give me a pain in the neck."

"I can understand that," Reverend Hopkins said. "I can even sympathize, but till somebody else volunteers for Joseph, you're stuck with it."

"Nobody's ever going to do that!" Elmer said. "I even offered Grady Baker fifty cents to be Joseph and he wouldn't do it. I'm going to have to be Joseph for the rest of my life!"

"Cheer up," Reverend Hopkins told him. "Maybe somebody will turn up."

I'll bet he didn't think the somebody would be Ralph Herdman.

"All right," Mother said, "Ralph will be our Joseph. Now, does anyone else want to volunteer for Mary?" Mother looked all around, trying to catch somebody's eye — *anybody's* eye. "Janet? . . . Roberta? . . . Alice, don't you want to volunteer this year?"

"No," Alice said, so low you could hardly hear her. "I don't want to."

110

Nobody volunteered to be Wise Men either, except Leroy, Claude, and Ollie Herdman.

So there was my mother, stuck with a Christmas pageant full of Herdmans in the main roles.

There was one Herdman left over, and one main role left over, and you didn't have to be very smart to figure out that Gladys was going to be the Angel of the Lord.

"What do I have to do?" Gladys wanted to know.

"The Angel of the Lord was the one who brought the good news to the shepherds," Mother said.

Right away all the shepherds began to wiggle around in their seats, figuring that any good news Gladys brought them would come with a smack in the teeth.

Charlie's friend Hobie Carmichael raised his hand and said, "I can't be a shepherd. We're going to Philadelphia."

"Why didn't you say so before?" Mother asked.

"I forgot."

Another kid said, "My mother doesn't want me to be a shepherd."

"Why not?" Mother said.

"I don't know. She just said don't be a shepherd."

One kid was honest. "Gladys Herdman hits too hard," he said.

"Why, Gladys isn't going to hit anybody!" Mother said. "What an idea! The Angel just visits the shepherds in the fields and tells them Jesus is born."

111

"And hits 'em," said the kid.

Of course he was right. You could just picture Gladys whamming shepherds left and right, but Mother said that was perfectly ridiculous.

"I don't want to hear another word about it," she said. "No shepherds may quit — or get sick," she added, before the kid in the front pew could ask.

While everybody was leaving, Mother grabbed Alice Wendleken by the arm and said, "Alice, why in the world didn't you raise your hand to be Mary?"

"I don't know," Alice said, looking mad.

But I knew — I'd heard Imogene Herdman telling Alice what would happen to her if she dared to volunteer: all the ordinary, everyday Herdman-things like clonking you on the head, and drawing pictures all over your homework papers, and putting worms in your coat pocket.

"I don't care," Alice told her. "I don't care what you do. I'm always Mary in the pageant."

"And next spring," Imogene went on, squinching up her eyes, "when the pussy willows come out, I'll stick a pussy willow so far down your ear that nobody can reach it — and it'll sprout there, and it'll grow and grow, and you'll spend the rest of your life with a pussy-willow bush growing out your ear."

You had to admire her — that was the worst thing any of them ever thought up to do. Of course some people might not think that could happen, but it could. Ollie Herdman did it once. He got this terrible earache in school, and when the nurse looked down his ear with her little lighted tube she yelled so loud you could hear her all the way down the hall. "He's got something growing down there!" she hollered.

They had to take Ollie to the hospital and put him under and dig this sprouted pussy willow out of his ear.

So that was why Alice kept her mouth shut about being Mary.

"You know she wouldn't do all those things she said," I told Alice as we walked home.

"Yes, she would," Alice said. "Herdmans will do anything. But your mother should have told them no. Somebody should put Imogene out of the pageant, and all the rest of them too. They'll do something terrible and ruin the whole thing."

I thought she was probably right, and so did lots of other people, and for two or three days all anybody could talk about was the Herdmans being Mary and Joseph and all.

Mrs. Homer McCarthy called Mother to say that she had been thinking and thinking about it, and if the Herdmans wanted to participate in our Christmas celebration, why didn't we let them hand out programs at the door?

"We don't have programs for the Christmas pageant," Mother said.

"Well, maybe we ought to get some printed and put the Herdmans in charge of that."

Alice's mother told the Ladies' Aid that it was sacrilegious to let Imogene Herdman be Mary. Somebody we never heard of called up Mother on the telephone and said her name was Hazelbeck and she lived on Sproul Hill, and was it true that Imogene Herdman was going to be Mary the mother of Jesus in a church play?

"Yes," Mother said. "Imogene is going to be Mary in our Christmas pageant."

"And the rest of them, too?" the lady asked.

"Yes, Ralph is going to be Joseph and the others are the Wise Men and the Angel of the Lord."

"You must be crazy," this Mrs. Hazelbeck told Mother. "I live next door to that outfit with their yelling and screaming and their insane cat and their garage door going up and down, up and down all day long, and let me tell you, you're in for a rowdy time!"

Some people said it wasn't fair for a whole family who didn't even go to our church to barge in and take over the pageant. My father said somebody better lock up the Women's Society's silver service. My mother just said she would rather be in the hospital with Mrs. Armstrong.

But then the flower committee took a potted geranium to Mrs. Armstrong and told her what was going on and she nearly fell out of bed, traction bars and all. "I feel personally responsible," she said. "Whatever happens, I accept the blame. If I'd been up and around and doing my duty, this never would have happened."

And that made my mother so mad she couldn't see straight.

"If she'd been up and around it wouldn't have happened!" Mother said. "That woman! She must be surprised that the sun is still coming up every morning without her to supervise the sunrise. Well, let me tell you —"

"Don't tell me," my father said. "I'm on your side."

"I just mean that Helen Armstrong is not the only woman alive who can run a Christmas pageant. Up till now I'd made up my mind just to do the best I could under the circumstances, but *now* —" She stabbed a meat fork into the pot roast. "I'm going to make this the very best Christmas pageant anybody ever saw, and I'm going to do it with Herdmans, too. After all, they raised their hands and nobody else did. And that's that."

And it was, too. For one thing, nobody else wanted to take over the pageant, with or without Herdmans; and for another thing, Reverend Hopkins got fed up with all the complaints and told everybody where to get off.

Of course, he didn't say "Go jump in the lake, Mrs. Wendleken" or anything like that. He just reminded everyone that when Jesus said "Suffer the little children to come unto me" Jesus meant all the little children, including Herdmans.

So that shut everybody up, even Alice's mother, and the next Wednesday we started rehearsals.

On the night of the pageant we didn't have any supper because Mother forgot to fix it. My father said that was all right. Between Mrs. Armstrong's telephone calls and the pageant rehearsals, he didn't expect supper anymore.

"When it's all over," he said, "we'll go someplace and have hamburgers." But Mother said when it was all over she might want to go someplace and hide.

"We've never once gone through the whole thing," she said. "I don't know what's going to happen. It may be the first Christmas pageant in history where Joseph and the Wise Men get in a fight, and Mary runs away with the baby."

She might be right, I thought, and I wondered what all of us in the angel choir ought to do in case that happened. It would be dumb for us just to stand there singing about the Holy Infant if Mary had run off with him.

But nothing seemed very different at first.

There was the usual big mess all over the place — baby angels getting poked in the eye by other baby angels' wings and grumpy shepherds stumbling over their bathrobes. The spotlight swooped back and forth and up and down till it made you sick at your stomach to look at it and, as usual, whoever was playing the piano pitched "Away in a Manger" so high we could hardly hear it, let alone sing it. My father says "Away in a Manger" always starts out sounding like a closetful of mice.

But everything settled down, and at 7:30 the pageant began.

While we sang "Away in a Manger," the ushers lit candles all around the church, and the spotlight came on to be the star. So you really had to know the words to "Away in a Manger" because you couldn't see anything — not even Alice Wendleken's vaseline eyelids.

After that we sang two verses of "O, Little Town of Bethlehem," and then we were supposed to hum some more "O, Little Town of Bethlehem" while Mary and Joseph came in from a side door. Only they didn't come right away. So we hummed and hummed and hummed, which is boring and also very hard, and before long doesn't sound like any song at all — more like an old refrigerator.

"I knew something like this would happen," Alice Wendleken whispered to me. "They didn't come at all! We won't have any Mary and Joseph — and now what are we supposed to do?"

I guess we would have gone on humming till we all turned blue, but we didn't have to. Ralph and Imogene

117

were there all right, only for once they didn't come through the door pushing each other out of the way. They just stood there for a minute as if they weren't sure they were in the right place — because of the candles, I guess, and the church being full of people. They looked like the people you see on the six o'clock news — refugees, sent to wait in some strange ugly place, with all their boxes and sacks around them.

It suddenly occurred to me that this was just the way it must have been for the real Holy Family, stuck away in a barn by people who didn't much care what happened to them. They couldn't have been very neat and tidy either, but more like *this* Mary and Joseph (Imogene's veil was cockeyed as usual, and Ralph's hair stuck out all around his ears). Imogene had the baby doll but she wasn't carrying it the way she was supposed to, cradled in her arms. She had it slung up over her shoulder, and before she put it in the manger she thumped it twice on the back.

I heard Alice gasp and she poked me. "I don't think it's very nice to burp the baby Jesus," she whispered, "as if he had colic." Then she poked me again. "Do you suppose he could have had colic?"

I said, "I don't know why not," and I didn't. He *could* have had colic, or been fussy, or hungry like any other baby. After all, that was the whole point of Jesus — that he didn't come down on a cloud like something out of

"Amazing Comics," but that he was born and lived . . . a real person.

Right away we had to sing "While Shepherds Watched Their Flocks by Night" — and we had to sing very loud, because there were more shepherds than there were anything else, and they made so much noise, banging their crooks around like a lot of hockey sticks.

Next came Gladys, from behind the angel choir, pushing people out of the way and stepping on everyone's feet. Since Gladys was the only one in the pageant who had anything to say she made the most of it: "Hey! Unto you a child is born!" she hollered, as if it was, for sure, the best news in the world. And all the shepherds trembled, sore afraid — of Gladys, mainly, but it looked good anyway.

Then came three carols about angels. It took that long to get the angels in because they were all primary kids and they got nervous and cried and forgot where they were supposed to go and bent their wings in the door and things like that.

We got a little rest then, while the boys sang "We Three Kings of Orient Are," and everybody in the audience shifted around to watch the Wise Men march up the aisle.

"What have they got?" Alice whispered.

I didn't know, but whatever it was, it was heavy — Leroy almost dropped it. He didn't have his frankincense jar either, and Claude and Ollie didn't have anything although they were supposed to bring the gold and the myrrh.

"I knew this would happen," Alice said for the second time. "I bet it's something awful."

"Like what?"

"Like . . . a burnt offering. You know the Herdmans."

Well, they did burn things, but they hadn't burned this yet. It was a ham — and right away I knew where it came from. My father was on the church charitable works committee — they give away food baskets at Christmas, and this was the Herdmans' food-basket ham. It still had the ribbon around it, saying Merry Christmas.

"I'll bet they stole that!" Alice said.

"They did not. It came from their food basket, and if they want to give away their own ham I guess they can do it." But even if the Herdmans didn't *like* ham (that was Alice's next idea) they had never before in their lives given anything away except lumps on the head. So you had to be impressed.

Leroy dropped the ham in front of the manger. It looked funny to see a ham there instead of the fancy bath-salts jars we always used for the myrrh and the frankincense. And then they went and sat down in the only space that was left.

While we sang "What Child Is This?" the Wise Men were supposed to confer among themselves and then leave by a different door, so everyone would understand that they were going home another way. But the

Herdmans forgot, or didn't want to, or something, because they didn't confer and they didn't leave either. They just sat there, and there wasn't anything anyone could do about it.

"They're ruining the whole thing!" Alice whispered, but they weren't at all. As a matter of fact, it made perfect sense for the Wise Men to sit down and rest, and I said so.

"They're supposed to have come a long way. You wouldn't expect them just to show up, hand over the ham, and leave!"

As for ruining the whole thing, it seemed to me that the Herdmans had improved the pageant a lot, just by doing what came naturally — like burping the baby, for instance, or thinking a ham would make a better present than a lot of perfumed oil.

Usually, by the time we got to "Silent Night," which was always the last carol, I was fed up with the whole thing and couldn't wait for it to be over. But I didn't feel that way this time. I almost wished for the pageant to go on, with the Herdmans in charge, to see what else they would do that was different.

Maybe the Wise Men would tell Mary about their problem with Herod, and she would tell them to go back and lie their heads off. Or Joseph might go with them and get rid of Herod once and for all. Or Joseph and Mary might ask the Wise Men to take the Christ Child with them, figuring that no one would think to look there.

I was so busy planning new ways to save the baby Jesus that I missed the beginning of "Silent Night," but it was all right because everyone sang "Silent Night," including the audience. We sang all the verses, too, and when we got to "Son of God, Love's pure light" I happened to look at Imogene and I almost dropped my hymn book on a baby angel.

Everyone had been waiting all this time for the Herdmans to do something absolutely unexpected. And sure enough, that was what happened.

Imogene Herdman was crying.

In the candlelight her face was all shiny with tears and she didn't even bother to wipe them away. She just sat there — awful old Imogene — in her crookedy veil, crying and crying.

Well. It *was* the best Christmas pageant we ever had.

From
My Side of the Mountain

Jean Craighead George

Young Sam Gribley grew tired of living in a crowded New York City apartment. He runs away to the wilderness of the Catskill Mountains to forge a life by himself. Armed with only a penknife, a ball of cord, forty dollars, and some flint and steel, Sam learns how to survive on his own. This selection from the Newbery Honor Book tells the story of Sam's first Christmas in the wild.

I looked at my calendar pole one day, and realized that it was almost Christmas. Bando will come, I thought. I'll have to prepare a feast and make a present for him. I took stock of the frozen venison and decided that there were enough steaks for us to eat nothing but venison for a month. I scooped under the snow for teaberry plants to boil down and pour over snowballs for dessert.

I checked my cache of wild onions to see if I had enough to make onion soup, and set aside some large firm groundnuts for mashed potatoes. There were still piles of dogtooth violet bulbs and Solomon's seal roots and a few dried apples. I cracked walnuts, hickory nuts, and beechnuts, then began a pair of deer-hide moccasins to be lined with rabbit fur for Bando's present. I finished these before Christmas, so I started a hat of the same materials.

Two days before Christmas I began to wonder if Bando would come. He had forgotten, I was sure — or he was busy, I said. Or he thought that I was no longer here and decided not to tramp out through the snows to find out.

On Christmas Eve Bando still had not arrived, and I began to plan for a very small Christmas with Frightful.

About four-thirty Christmas Eve I hung a small red cluster of teaberries on the deerskin door. I went in my tree room for a snack of beechnuts when I heard a faint "halloooo" from far down the mountain. I snuffed out my tallow candle, jumped into my coat and moccasins, and plunged out into the snow. Again a "halloooo" floated over the quiet snow. I took a bearing on the sound and bounced down the hill to meet Bando. I ran into him just as he turned up the valley to follow the stream bed. I was so glad to see him that I hugged him and pounded him on the back.

"Never thought I'd make it," he said. "I walked all the way from the entrance of the State Park; pretty good, eh?" He smiled and slapped his tired legs. Then he grabbed my arm, and with three quick pinches, tested the meat on me.

"You've been living well," he said. He looked closely at my face. "But you're gonna need a shave in a year or two." I thanked him and we sprang up the mountain, cut across through the gorge and home.

"How's the Frightful?" he asked as soon as we were inside and the light was lit.

I whistled. She jumped to my fist. He got bold and stroked her. "And the jam?" he asked.

"Excellent, except the crocks are absorbent and are sopping up all the juice."

"Well, I brought you some more sugar; we'll try next year. Merry Christmas, Thoreau!" he shouted, and looked about the room.

"I see you have been busy. A blanket, new clothes, and an ingenious fireplace — with a real chimney — and say, you have silverware!" He picked up the forks I had carved.

We ate smoked fish for dinner with boiled dogtooth violet bulbs. Walnuts dipped in jam were dessert. Bando was pleased with his jam.

When we were done, Bando stretched out on my bed. He propped his feet up and lit his pipe.

"And now, I have something to show you," he said. He reached in his coat pocket and took out a newspaper clipping. It was from a New York paper, and it read:

WILD BOY SUSPECTED LIVING OFF DEER
AND NUTS IN WILDERNESS OF CATSKILLS

I looked at Bando and leaned over to read the headline myself.

"Have you been talking?" I asked.

"Me? Don't be ridiculous. You have had several visitors other than me."

"The fire warden — the old lady!" I cried out.

"Now, Thoreau, this could only be a rumor. Just because it is in print, doesn't mean it's true. Before you get excited, sit still and listen." He read:

"'Residents of Delhi, in the Catskill Mountains, report that a wild boy, who lives off deer and nuts, is hiding out in the mountains.

"'Several hunters stated that this boy stole deer from them during hunting season.'"

"I did not!" I shouted. "I only took the ones they had wounded and couldn't find."

"Well, that's what they told their wives when they came home without their deer. Anyway, listen to this:

"'This wild boy has been seen from time to time by Catskill residents, some of whom believe he is crazy!'"

"Well, that's a terrible thing to say!"

"Just awful," he stated. "Any normal red-blooded American boy wants to live in a tree house and trap his own food. They just don't do it, that's all."

"Read on," I said.

"'Officials say that there is no evidence of any boy living alone in the mountains, and add that all abandoned houses and sheds are routinely checked for just such events. Nevertheless, the residents are sure that such a boy exists!' End of story."

"That's a lot of nonsense!" I leaned back against the bedstead and smiled.

"Ho, ho, don't think that ends it," Bando said, and reached in his pocket for another clipping. "This one is dated December fifth, the other was November twenty-third. Shall I read?"

"Yes."

128

OLD WOMAN REPORTS MEETING WILD BOY
WHILE PICKING STRAWBERRIES IN CATSKILLS

"'Mrs. Thomas Fielder, ninety-seven, resident of Delhi, N.Y., told this reporter that she met a wild boy on Bitter Mountain last June while gathering her annual strawberry jelly supply.

"'She said the boy was brown-haired, dusty, and wandering aimlessly around the mountains. However, she added, he seemed to be in good flesh and happy.

"'The old woman, a resident of the mountain resort town for ninety-seven years, called this office to report her observation. Local residents report that Mrs. Fielder is a fine old member of the community, who only occasionally sees imaginary things.'"

Bando roared. I must say I was sweating, for I really did not expect this turn of events.

"And now," went on Bando, "and now the queen of the New York papers. This story was buried on page nineteen. No sensationalism for this paper.

BOY REPORTED LIVING OFF LAND IN CATSKILLS

"'A young boy of seventeen or eighteen, who left home with a group of Boy Scouts, is reported to be still scouting in that area, according to the fire warden of the Catskill Mountains.

"'Evidence of someone living in the forest — a fire-

129

place, soup bones, and cracked nuts — was reported by Warden Jim Handy, who spent the night in the wilderness looked for the lad. Jim stated that the young man had apparently left the area, as there was no evidence of his camp upon a second trip — ' "

"What second trip?" I asked.

Bando puffed his pipe, looked at me wistfully and said, "Are you ready to listen?"

"Sure," I answered.

"Well, here's the rest of it, ' . . . there was no trace of his camp on a second trip, and the warden believes that the young man returned to his home at the end of the summer.'

"You know, Thoreau, I could scarcely drag myself away from the newspapers to come up here. You make a marvelous story."

I said, "Put more wood on the fire, it is Christmas. No one will be searching these mountains until May Day."

Bando asked for the willow whistles. I got them for him, and after running the scale several times, he said, "Let us serenade the ingenuity of the American newspaperman. Then let us serenade the conservationists who have protected the American wilderness, so that a boy can still be alone in this world of millions of people."

I thought that was suitable, and we played "Holy Night." We tried "The Twelve Days of Christmas," but the whistles were too stiff and Bando too tired.

"Thoreau, my body needs rest. Let's give up," he said

after two bad starts. I banked the fire and blew out the candle and slept in my clothes.

It was Christmas when we awoke. Breakfast was light — acorn pancakes, jam, and sassafras tea. Bando went for a walk, I lit the fire in the fireplace and spent the morning creating a feast from the wilderness.

I gave Bando his presents when he returned. He liked them. He was really pleased; I could tell by his eyebrows. They went up and down and in and out. Furthermore, I know he liked the presents because he wore them.

The onion soup was about to be served when I heard a voice shouting in the distance, "I know you are there! I know you are there! Where are you?"

"*Dad!*" I screamed, and dove right through the door onto my stomach. I all but fell down the mountain shouting, "Dad! Dad! Where are you?" I found him resting in a snowdrift, looking at the cardinal pair that lived near the stream. He was smiling, stretched out on his back, not in exhaustion, but in joy.

"Merry Christmas!" he whooped. I ran toward him. He jumped to his feet, tackled me, thumped my chest, and rubbed snow in my face.

Then he stood up, lifted me from the snow by the pockets on my coat, and held me off the ground so that we were eye to eye. He sure smiled. He threw me down in the snow again and wrestled with me for a few minutes. Our formal greeting done, we strode up the mountain.

"Well, son," he began. "I've been reading about you in the papers and I could no longer resist the temptation to visit you. I still can't believe you did it."

His arm went around me. He looked real good, and I was overjoyed to see him.

"How did you find me?" I asked eagerly.

"I went to Mrs. Fielder, and she told me which mountain. At the stream I found your raft and ice-fishing holes. Then I looked for trails and footsteps. When I thought I was getting warm, I hollered."

"Am I that easy to find?"

"You didn't have to answer, and I'd probably have frozen in the snow." He was pleased and not angry at me at all. He said again, "I just didn't think you'd do it. I was sure you'd be back the next day. When you weren't, I bet on the next week; then the next month. How's it going?"

"Oh, it's a wonderful life, Dad!"

When we walked into the tree, Bando was putting the final touches on the venison steak.

"Dad, this is my friend, Professor Bando; he's a teacher. He got lost one day last summer and stumbled onto my camp. He liked it so well that he came back for Christmas. Bando, meet my father."

Bando turned the steak on the spit, rose, and shook my father's hand.

"I am pleased to meet the man who sired this boy," he said grandly. I could see that they liked each other and that it was going to be a splendid Christmas. Dad stretched out on the bed and looked around.

"I thought maybe you'd pick a cave," he said. "The papers reported that they were looking for you in old sheds and houses, but I knew better than that. However, I never would have thought of the inside of a tree. What a beauty! Very clever, son, very, very clever. This is a comfortable bed."

He noticed my food caches, stood and peered into them. "Got enough to last until spring?"

"I think so," I said. "If I don't keep getting hungry visitors all the time." I winked at him.

"Well, I would wear out my welcome by a year if I could, but I have to get back to work soon after Christmas."

"How's Mom and all the rest?" I asked as I took down the turtle-shell plates and set them on the floor.

"She's marvelous. How she manages to feed and clothe those eight youngsters on what I bring her, I don't know; but she does it. She sends her love, and says that she hopes you are eating well-balanced meals."

The onion soup was simmering and ready. I gave Dad his.

"First course," I said.

He breathed deeply of the odor and downed it boiling hot.

"Son, this is better onion soup than the chef at the Waldorf can make."

Bando sipped his, and I put mine in the snow to cool.

"Your mother will stop worrying about your diet when she hears of this."

Bando rinsed Dad's soup bowl in the snow, and with great ceremony and elegance — he could really be elegant when the occasion arose — poured him a turtle shell of sassafras tea. Quoting a passage from one of Dickens's food-eating scenes, he carved the blackened steak. It was pink and juicy inside. Cooked to perfection. We were all proud of it. Dad had to finish his tea before he could eat. I was short on bowls. Then I filled his shell. A mound of sort of fluffy mashed cattail tubers, mushrooms, and dogtooth violet bulbs, smothered in gravy thickened with acorn powder. Each plate had a pile of soaked and stewed honey locust beans — mixed with hickory nuts. The beans are so hard it took three days to soak them.

It was a glorious feast. Everyone was impressed, including me. When we were done, Bando went down to the stream and cut some old dried and hollow reeds. He came back and carefully made us each a flute with the tip of his penknife. He said the willow whistles were too old for such an occasion. We all played Christmas carols until dark. Bando wanted to try some complicated jazz tunes, but the late hour, the small fire dancing and throwing heat, and the snow insulating us from the winds made us all so sleepy that we were not capable of more than a last slow rendition of taps before we put ourselves on and under skins and blew out the light.

Before anyone was awake the next morning, I heard Frightful call hungrily. I had put her outside to sleep, as we were very crowded. I went out to find her. Her Christmas dinner had been a big piece of venison, but the night air had enlarged her appetite. I called her to my fist and we went into the meadow to rustle up breakfast for the guests. She was about to go after a rabbit, but I thought that wasn't proper fare for a post-Christmas breakfast, so we went to the stream. Frightful caught herself a pheasant while I kicked a hole in the ice and did a little ice fishing. I caught about six trout and whistled Frightful to my hand. We returned to the hemlock. Dad and Bando were still asleep, with their feet in each other's faces, but both looking very content.

I built the fire and was cooking the fish and making pancakes when Dad shot out of bed.

"Wild boy!" he shouted. "What a sanguine smell. What a purposeful fire. Breakfast in a tree. Son, I toil from sunup to sundown, and never have I lived so well!"

I served him. He choked a bit on the acorn pancakes — they are a little flat and hard — but Bando got out some of his blueberry jam and smothered the pancakes with an enormous portion. Dad went through the motions of eating this. The fish, however, he enjoyed, and he asked for more. We drank sassafras tea, sweetened with some of the sugar Bando had brought me, rubbed our turtle shells clean in the snow, and went out into the forest.

Dad had not met Frightful. When she winged down out of the hemlock, he ducked and flattened out in the snow shouting, "Blast off."

He was very cool toward Frightful until he learned that she was the best provider we had ever had in our family, and then he continually praised her beauty and admired her talents. He even tried to pet her, but Frightful was not to be won. She snagged him with her talons.

They stayed away from each other for the rest of Dad's visit, although Dad never ceased to admire her from a safe distance.

Bando had to leave two or three days after Christmas. He had some papers to grade, and he started off reluctantly one morning, looking very unhappy about the way of life he had chosen. He shook hands all around and then turned to me and said, "I'll save all the newspaper clippings for you, and if the reporters start getting too hot on your trail, I'll call the New York papers and give them a bum steer." I could see he rather liked the idea, and departed a little happier.

Dad lingered on for a few more days, ice fishing, setting my traps and snares, and husking walnuts. He whittled some cooking spoons and forks.

On New Year's Day he announced that he must go.

"I told your mother I would only stay for Christmas. It's a good thing she knows me or she might be worried."

"She won't send the police out to look for you?" I asked hurriedly. "Could she think you never found me?"

"Oh, I told her I'd call her Christmas night if I didn't." He poked around for another hour or two, trying to decide just how to leave. Finally he started down the mountain. He had hardly gone a hundred feet before he was back.

"I've decided to leave by another route. Somebody might backtrack me and find you. And that would be too bad." He came over to me and put his hand on my shoulder. "You've done very well, Sam." He grinned and walked off toward the gorge.

From
Santa Paws

Nicholas Edwards

A poor stray dog wanders into town one Christmas season and wherever he goes, he seems to help people. He helps an old woman who has fallen and broken her hip, and he saves a little boy from drowning in a mall fountain. Everyone calls the heroic dog Santa Paws, but all he wants is a home and a family to love him. Siblings Gregory and Patricia want to bring him home — if they can find him.

*G*regory and Oscar met on the school playground at ten-thirty. Patricia had insisted on coming along, too. Since the food was gone and the towels in the cardboard box were rumpled, they knew that the dog had been there. But he was gone now — and they had no way of knowing if he would ever come back.

"Where does he *go* every day?" Gregory asked, frustrated. "Doesn't he want us to find him?"

Oscar shrugged as he opened a brand-new can of Alpo stew. "He's off doing hero stuff, probably."

Patricia didn't like to see the towels looking so messy. She bent down to refold them. "You know, that was really something at the mall," she remarked. "I've never seen a dog do anything like that before."

"He's not just any dog," Gregory said proudly.

Patricia nodded. For once, her brother was right. "I have to say, it was pretty cool." She reached into the open Milk-Bone box. "How many should I leave him?"

"Three," Gregory told her. "In a nice, neat row."

"Since it's Christmas Eve, let's give him four," Oscar suggested.

"Sounds good," Patricia said, and took out four biscuits.

When they were done, they sat down on a wool blanket Oscar had brought. It was much more pleasant than sitting in the cold snow. Mrs. Callahan had packed them a picnic lunch, too.

So they spent the next couple of hours eating sandwiches, drinking out of juice boxes, and playing cards. Patricia hated Hearts, so mostly they played inept poker.

"Is this going to get any more interesting?" Patricia asked at one point.

Gregory and Oscar shook their heads.

"Great," Patricia said grumpily. Then she slouched down to deal another hand of cards. "Aces wild, boys. Place your bets."

They waited and waited, but the dog never showed up. They had stayed so long that the batteries in Gregory's portable tape deck were running down.

"Is it okay if we go now?" Patricia asked. "I'm *really* tired of playing cards."

"Me, too," Oscar confessed.

"We might as well," Gregory said with a sigh. He was pretty sick of cards, too. "I don't think he's coming." He reached for a small plastic bag and started collecting all of their trash. "Do you think Mom and Dad would let us come here at night? Maybe we'd find him here, asleep."

"They wouldn't let us come *alone*," Patricia said. "But if we asked really nicely, they might come with us. I mean, they're the ones who are always telling us to be kind to animals, right?"

Gregory nodded. His parents had always *stressed* the importance of being kind to animals.

"You should write down what you're going to say first," Oscar advised them. He never really liked to leave things to chance. In the Cub Scouts, he had learned a lot about being prepared. "That way, you can practice how you're going to do it. Work out all the bugs."

"Let me write it," Patricia told her brother. "I have a bigger vocabulary."

Gregory just shrugged. All he wanted to do was find the dog — one way or another.

He was beginning to be afraid that the dog didn't *want* to be found.

Hours passed before the dog regained consciousness. It was well past midnight, and the woods were pitch-black. His shoulder had stiffened so much that at first, he couldn't get up. But finally, he staggered to his feet. He wanted to lie right back down, but he made himself stay up.

He stood there, swaying. He felt dizzy and sick. What he wanted right now, more than anything, was to be inside that warm cardboard box, sleeping on those soft towels that smelled so clean and fresh.

He limped out to the road, whimpering every time his bad leg hit the ground. The bleeding had stopped, but now that he was moving around, it started up again.

The only way he was going to make it back to the school was if he put one foot after the other. He limped painfully up the road, staring down at his front paws the whole way. One step. Two. Three. Four. It was hard work.

Whenever possible, he took shortcuts. He cut through alleys, and parking lots, and backyards. The lights were off all over town. People were sound asleep, dreaming about Christmas morning. The dog just staggered along, putting one foot in front of the other. Over and over.

He was plodding through someone's front yard when he felt the hair on his back rise. Oh, now what? He was *too tired*. But — he smelled smoke! Even though he was dizzy, he lifted his head to sniff the air. Where was it coming from?

He followed the trail across several yards and up to a yellow two-story house. Smoke was billowing out through a crack in the living room window. Someone had left the Christmas tree lights on, and the tree had ignited! The lights were snapping and popping, and the ornaments were bursting into flames. He could hear the crackle of electricity, and smell the smoke getting stronger.

The house was on fire!

He lurched up the front steps and onto the porch. He

was too weak to paw on the door, but he *could* still bark. He threw his head back and howled into the silent night. He barked and barked until the other dogs in the neighborhood woke up and started joining in. Soon, there were dogs howling and yapping everywhere.

After a few minutes of that, lights started going on in houses up and down the block. The dog was losing strength, but he kept barking. Why didn't the people come outside? Didn't they know that their house was burning?

The living room windows were getting black from the smoke, as the fire spread. Why wouldn't the people wake up? Maybe he was going to have to go in and *get* them. But how?

He started throwing his body feebly against the front door, but it wouldn't budge. Why couldn't the people hear him barking? Where were they? If they didn't wake up soon, they might die from the smoke!

The dog limped to the farthest end of the porch, trying to gather up all of his strength. Then he raced towards the living room window and threw himself into the glass at full speed. The window shattered and he landed in the middle of the burning room. He was covered with little shards of glass, but he didn't have time to shake them off. He had to go find the family! The floor was very hot, and he burned the bottom of his paws as he ran across the room. It was scary in here!

The doorway was blocked by fire, but he launched

himself up into the air and soared through the flames. He could smell burned fur where his coat had been singed, but he ignored that and limped up the stairs as fast as he could. He kept barking and howling the entire way, trying to sound the alarm. A burning ember had fallen onto his back and he yelped when he felt the pain, but then he just went back to barking.

A man came stumbling out of the master bedroom in a pair of flannel pajamas. It was Mr. Brown, who lived in the house with his wife and two daughters, and he was weak from smoke inhalation.

"Wh-what's going on?" Mr. Brown mumbled. "It's the middle of the —"

The dog barked, and tugged at his pajama leg with his teeth, trying to pull him down the stairs.

Mr. Brown saw the flames downstairs and gasped. "Fire!" he yelled, and ran into his children's bedroom. "Wake up, everyone! The house is on fire!"

The dog ran into the master bedroom, barking as loudly as he could until Mrs. Brown groggily climbed out of bed. She was coughing from the smoke, and seemed very confused. The dog barked, and nudged her towards the door.

Mr. Brown rushed down the stairs with his two sleepy children and a squirming Siamese cat, and then went back for his wife. By now, she was only steps behind him, carrying a cage full of gerbils.

The dog was exhausted, but he kept barking until

they were all safely outside. Once he was sure the house was empty, he staggered out to the yard, his lungs and eyes hurting from the thick smoke. He sank down in the snow, coughing and gagging and quivering from fear.

One of the neighbors had called 911, and the first fire engine was just arriving. The firefighters leaped out, carrying various pieces of equipment and grabbing lengths of hose. By now, the fire had spread from the living room to the dining room.

"Is anyone still in there?" the engine company lieutenant yelled.

"No," Mrs. Brown answered, coughing from the smoke she had inhaled. "It's okay! We all got out."

Because they had been called only a minute or two after the fire started, the fire department was able to put the fire out quickly. Although the living room and dining room were destroyed, the rest of the house had been saved. Instead of losing everything, including their lives, the Browns would still have a place to live.

During all of this, the dog had limped over to the nearest bush. He crawled underneath it as far as he could go. Then he collapsed in exhaustion. His injured shoulder was throbbing, he was still gagging, and all he could smell was smoke. His paws hurt, and he licked at the pads, trying to get rid of the burning sensation. They hurt so much that he couldn't stop whimpering. His back was stinging from where the ember had hit it, and he had lots of new cuts from leaping through the glass.

He huddled into a small ball, whimpering to himself. He had never been in so much pain in his life.

While the other firefighters checked to make sure that the fire was completely out, the chief went over to interview Mr. and Mrs. Brown. The Oceanport Fire Department was staffed by volunteers, and Fire Chief Jefferson had run the department for many years.

"How did you get out?" Chief Jefferson asked, holding an incident report form and a ballpoint pen. "Did your smoke detector wake you up?"

Mr. and Mrs. Brown exchanged embarrassed glances.

"We, um, kind of took the battery out a few days ago," Mr. Brown mumbled. "See, the remote control went dead, and . . ." His voice trailed off.

"We were going to get another battery for the smoke detector," Mrs. Brown said, coming to his defense. "But, with the holidays and all, we just —"

"Hadn't gotten around to it yet," Chief Jefferson finished the sentence for her.

The Browns nodded, and looked embarrassed.

Chief Jefferson sighed. "Well, then, all I can say is that you were very lucky. On a windy night like tonight, a fire can get out of control in no time."

Mr. and Mrs. Brown and their daughters nodded solemnly. They knew that they had had a very close call.

"So, what happened?" Chief Jefferson asked. "Did you smell the smoke?"

The Browns shook their heads.

"We were all asleep," Mrs. Brown said.

Chief Jefferson frowned. "Then I don't understand what happened. Who woke you up?"

The Browns looked at one another.

"It was Santa Paws!" they all said in unison. "Who else?"

It was Christmas morning, and the Callahans were getting ready to go to church. On Christmas Eve, they had gone over to the Oceanport Hospital maternity ward to visit their brand-new niece. Mr. Callahan's brother Steve and his wife, Emily, had had a beautiful baby girl named Miranda. Gregory and Patricia thought she was kind of red and wrinkly, but on the whole, pretty cute.

On the way home, they talked their parents into stopping at the middle school. But when they went to the little alcove, the food and water dishes hadn't been touched. The towels were still neatly folded, too. For some reason, the dog had never returned. Maybe he was gone for good.

Gregory knew that something terrible must have happened to him, but right now, there wasn't anything he could do about it. As far as he knew, no one had seen the dog since he had found Rachel's wallet that morning. And that was *hours* ago. Now, for all Gregory knew, the dog could be lying somewhere, alone, and scared, and *hurt*.

His father put his hand on his shoulder. "Come on,

Greg," he said gently. "It'll be okay. We'll come back again tomorrow."

Gregory nodded, and followed his family back to the car.

They went home and ate cookies and listened to Christmas carols. Mrs. Callahan made popcorn. Mr. Callahan read *The Night Before Christmas* aloud. Patricia told complicated jokes, and Gregory pretended that he thought they were funny. Then they all went to bed.

Gregory didn't get much sleep. He was too upset. Deep inside, he knew that the dog was gone for good. He was sure that he would never see him again — and the thought of that made him feel like crying.

When he got up, even though it was Christmas Day, he was more sad than excited. He and his father both put on suits and ties to wear to church. His mother and Patricia wore long skirts and festive blouses. Patricia also braided red and green ribbons into her hair.

Every year, on Christmas morning, there was a special, nonreligious, interdenominational service in Oceanport. No matter what holiday they celebrated, everyone in town was invited. This year, the service was being held at the Catholic church, but Rabbi Gladstone was going to be the main speaker. Next year, the service would be at the Baptist church, and the Methodist minister would lead the ceremony. As Father Reilly always said, it wasn't about religion, it was about *community*. It was about *neighbors*.

"Come on, Gregory," Mrs. Callahan said as they got into the station wagon. "Cheer up. It's Christmas."

Gregory nodded, and did his best to smile. Inside, though, he was miserable.

"When we get home, we have all those presents to open," Patricia reminded him. "And I spent *a lot* of money on yours."

Gregory smiled again, feebly.

The church was very crowded. Almost the entire town had shown up. People were smiling, and waving, and shaking hands with each other. There was a definite feeling of goodwill in the air. Oceanport was *always* a friendly and tolerant town, but the holiday season was special.

Gregory sat in his family's pew with his eyes closed and his hands tightly folded. He was wishing with all of his heart that the dog was okay. No matter how hard he tried, he couldn't seem to feel *any* Christmas spirit. How could he believe in the magic of Christmas, if he couldn't even save one little stray dog?

Rabbi Gladstone stepped up to the podium in the front of the church. "Welcome, everyone," he said. "Season's greetings to all of you!"

Then, the service began.

After the fire had been put out and the Browns had gone across the street to stay with neighbors, the dog was alone underneath his bush. He dragged himself deeper into the woods, whimpering softly. He knew he was badly hurt, and that he needed help.

He crawled through the woods until he couldn't make it any further. Then he lay down on his side in the snow. He stayed in that same position all night long. By now, he was too exhausted even to *whimper*.

In the morning, he made himself get up. If he stayed here by himself, he might die. Somehow, he had to make it back to the school. If he could do that, maybe his friends Gregory and Oscar would come and help him. He *needed* help, desperately.

Each limping step was harder than the one before, and the dog had to force himself to keep going. The town seemed to be deserted. He limped down Main Street, undisturbed.

The park was empty, too. The dog staggered across the wide expanse, falling down more than once. He was cold, he was in pain, and he was *exhausted*.

Naturally, he was also hungry.

When he tottered past the church, he paused at the bottom of the stairs. The doors were open and welcoming, warm air rushed out at him. For days, he had been trying to *give* help. Maybe now it was time to *get* some.

He dragged himself up the steps. His shoulder throbbed and burned with pain the entire way. When he got to the top, he was panting heavily. Could he make it any further, or should he just fall down right here?

He could smell lots of people. Too many people. Too

many different scents. Some of the scents were familiar, but he was too confused to sort them all out. *Walking* took up all of his energy.

He hobbled into the church, weaving from side to side. He started down the center aisle, and then his bad leg gave out under his weight. He fell on the floor and then couldn't get up again. He let his head slump forward against his front paws and then closed his eyes.

A hush fell over the church.

"I don't believe it," someone said, sounding stunned. "It's Santa Paws!"

Now that the silence had been broken, everyone started talking at once.

Hearing the name "Santa Paws," Gregory sat up straight in his pew. Then he stood up so he could see better.

"That's my dog," he whispered, so excited that he was barely able to breathe. "Look at my poor dog!" Then he put his pinkies in his mouth, and let out — noisy *air*.

Sitting next to him, Patricia sighed deeply. "*Really*, Greg," she said, and shook her head with grave disappointment. "Is that the best you can do?" She sighed again. Then she stuck her fingers in her mouth, and sent out a sharp, clear, and *earsplitting* whistle.

Instantly, the dog lifted his head. His ears shot up, and his tail began to rise.

"That's my dog!" Gregory shouted. He climbed past his parents and stumbled out into the aisle.

The dog was still too weak to get up, but he waved his tail as Gregory ran over to him.

"Are you all right?" Gregory asked, fighting back tears. "Don't worry, I'll take care of you. You're safe now."

Everyone in the church started yelling at once, and trying to crowd around the injured dog.

Patricia lifted her party skirt up a few inches so that she wouldn't trip on it. Then she stepped delicately into the aisle on her bright red holiday high heels.

"Quiet, please," she said in her most commanding voice. Then she raised her hands for silence. "Is there a veterinarian in the house?"

A man and a woman sitting in different sections of the church each stood up.

"Good." Patricia motioned for them both to come forward. "Step aside, please, everyone, and let them through."

A few people did as she said, but there was still a large, concerned group hovering around Gregory and the dog. The veterinarians were trying to get through, but the aisle was jammed.

Patricia's whistle was even more piercing this time. "I *said*," she repeated herself in a no-nonsense voice, "please step aside, in an orderly fashion."

The people standing in this aisle meekly did as they were told.

Watching all of this from their pew, Mr. Callahan leaned over to his wife.

"Do you get the sudden, sinking feeling that someday, we're going to have another cop in the family?" he asked.

Mrs. Callahan laughed. "I've had that feeling since she was *two*," she answered.

Gregory waited nervously as the two veterinarians examined the dog.

"Don't worry," the female vet announced after a couple of minutes. "He's going to be just fine."

Her colleague nodded. "Once we get him cleaned up and bandaged, and put in a few stitches, he'll be as good as new!"

Everyone in the church started clapping.

"Hooray for Santa Paws!" someone yelled.

"Merry Christmas, and God bless us everyone!" a little boy in the front row contributed.

Mr. Callahan leaned over to his wife again. "If that kid is holding a crutch, I'm *out* of here."

Mrs. Callahan grinned. "That's just Nathanial Haversham. His parents are *actors*."

"Oh." Mr. Callahan looked relieved. "Good."

Up in the front of the church, Rabbi Gladstone tapped on the microphone to get everyone's attention. Gradually, the church quieted down.

"Thank you," he said. "I think that this week, we've all seen proof that there *can* be holiday miracles. Even when it's hard to believe in magic, wonderful, unexplained things can still happen. That dog — an ordinary dog — has been saving lives and helping people throughout this season." He smiled in the dog's direction. "Thank you, and welcome to Oceanport, Santa Paws!"

Gregory didn't want to be rude, but he had to speak up. "Um, I'm sorry, Rabbi, but that's not his name," he said shyly.

"Whew," Patricia said, and pretended to wipe her arm across her forehead. "Promise me you're not going to call him Brownie, or Muffin, or anything else *cute*."

Gregory nodded. If he came up with a cute name, his sister would never let him live it down. Somehow, the name would have to be *cool*.

"What *is* his name, son?" Rabbi Gladstone asked kindly from the podium.

Gregory blinked a few times. His mind was a complete blank. "Well, uh, it's uh —"

"Sparky!" Oscar shouted, sitting with his family several rows away.

Everyone laughed.

"It's *not* Sparky," Gregory assured them. "It's, uh —"

"Solomon's a very nice name," Rabbi Gladstone suggested. "Isaiah has a nice ring to it, too."

Now, everyone in the church started shouting out different ideas. Names like Hero, and Rex, and Buttons.

"Oh, yeah, *Buttons*," Patricia said under her breath. "Like we wouldn't be totally humiliated to have a dog named *Buttons*."

Other names were suggested. Champ, and Sport, and Dasher, and Dancer. Frank, and Foxy, and Bud.

Bud?

Gregory looked at his dog for a long time. The dog wagged his tail and then lifted his paw into his new owner's lap. Gregory thought some more, and then, out of nowhere, it came to him. After all, what was another name for Santa Claus?

"His name's Nicholas," he told everyone. Then he smiled proudly and shook his dog's paw. "We call him *Nick*."

The dog barked and wagged his tail.

Then, Gregory stood up. "Come on, Nicky," he said. "It's time to go home."

The dog got up, too, balancing on three legs. He wagged his tail as hard as he could, and pressed his muzzle into Gregory's hand. He had a new owner, he had a new home, and he was going to have a whole new life.

He could hardly wait to get started!

From
A Christmas Memory,
One Christmas &
The Thankgiving Visitor

Truman Capote

Truman Capote was an American writer who is probably best known for his short novel Breakfast at Tiffany's. A Christmas Memory *is a memoir of the author's childhood, during which Capote, or "Buddy," lived with distant relatives in rural Alabama. This selection recalls a happy Christmas spent with his eccentric maiden aunt and best friend, Sook, and their dog, Queenie. Together, they created one wonderful Christmas with little money and lots of heart.*

"*I* know where we'll find real pretty trees, Buddy. And holly, too. With berries big as your eyes. It's way off in the woods. Farther than we've ever been. Papa used to bring us Christmas trees from there: carry them on his shoulder. That's fifty years ago. Well, now: I can't wait for morning."

Morning. Frozen rime lusters the grass; the sun, round as an orange and orange as hot-weather moons, balances on the horizon, burnishes the silvered winter woods. A wild turkey calls. A renegade hog grunts in the undergrowth. Soon, by the edge of knee-deep, rapid-running water, we have to abandon the buggy. Queenie wades the stream first, paddles across barking complaints at the swiftness of the current, the pneumonia-making coldness of it. We follow, holding our shoes and equipment (a hatchet, a burlap sack) above our heads. A mile more: of chastising thorns, burs and briers that catch at our clothes; of rusty pine needles brilliant with gaudy fungus and molted feathers. Here, there, a flash, a flutter, an ecstasy of shrillings remind us that not all the birds have flown south. Always, the path unwinds through lemony sun pools and pitch-black vine tunnels. Another creek to cross: a disturbed armada of speckled trout froths the water round us, and frogs the size of plates practice belly flops; beaver workmen are building a dam. On the farther shore, Queenie shakes herself and trembles. My friend shivers, too: not with cold but enthusiasm. One of her hat's ragged roses sheds a petal as she lifts her head and inhales the pine-heavy air. "We're almost there; can you smell it, Buddy?" she says, as though we were approaching an ocean.

And, indeed, it is a kind of ocean. Scented acres of holiday trees, prickly-leafed holly. Red berries shiny as Chinese bells: black crows swoop upon them screaming. Having stuffed our burlap sacks with enough greenery and crimson to garland a dozen windows, we set about choosing a tree. "It should be," muses my friend, "twice as tall as a boy. So a boy can't steal the star." The one we pick is twice as tall as me. A brave handsome brute that survives thirty hatchet strokes before it keels with a creaking rending cry. Lugging it like a kill, we commence the long trek out. Every few yards we abandon the struggle, sit down and pant. But we have the strength of triumphant huntsmen; that and the tree's virile, icy perfume revive us, goad us on. Many compliments accompany our sunset return along the red clay road to town; but my friend is sly and noncommittal when passers-by praise the treasure perched in our buggy: what a fine tree and where did it come from? "Yonderways," she murmurs vaguely. Once a car stops and the rich mill owner's lazy wife leans out and whines: "Giveya two-bits cash for that ol tree." Ordinarily my friend is afraid of saying no; but on this occasion she promptly shakes her head: "We wouldn't take a dollar." The mill owner's wife persists. "A dollar, my foot! Fifty cents. That's my last offer. Goodness, woman, you can get another one." In answer, my friend gently reflects: "I doubt it. There's never two of anything."

Home: Queenie slumps by the fire and sleeps till tomorrow, snoring loud as a human.

A trunk in the attic contains: a shoebox of ermine tails (off the opera cape of a curious lady who once rented a room in the house), coils of frazzled tinsel gone gold with age, one silver star, a brief rope of dilapidated, undoubtedly dangerous candy-like light bulbs. Excellent decorations, as far as they go, which isn't far enough: my friend wants our tree to blaze "like a Baptist window," droop with weighty snows of ornament. But we can't afford the made-in-Japan splendors at the five-and-dime. So we do what we've always done: sit for days at the kitchen table with scissors and crayons and stacks of colored paper. I make sketches and my friend cuts them out: lots of cats, fish too (because they're easy to draw), some apples, some watermelons, a few winged angels devised from saved-up sheets of Hershey-bar tin foil.

We use safety pins to attach these creations to the tree; as a final touch, we sprinkle the branches with shredded cotton (picked in August for this purpose). My friend, surveying the effect, clasps her hands together. "Now honest, Buddy. Doesn't it look good enough to eat?" Queenie tries to eat an angel.

After weaving and ribboning holly wreaths for all the front windows, our next project is the fashioning of family gifts. Tie-dye scarves for the ladies, for the men a home-brewed lemon and licorice and aspirin syrup to be taken "at the first Symptoms of a Cold and after Hunting." But when it comes time for making each other's gift, my friend and I separate to work secretly. I would like to buy her a pearl-handled knife, a radio, a whole pound of chocolate-covered cherries (we tasted some once and she always swears: "I could live on them, Buddy, Lord yes I could — and that's not taking His name in vain"). Instead, I am building her a kite. She would like to give me a bicycle (she's said so on several million occasions: "If only I could, Buddy. It's bad enough in life to do without something *you* want; but confound it, what gets my goat is not being able to give somebody something you want *them* to have. Only one of these days I will, Buddy. Locate you a bike. Don't ask how. Steal it, maybe"). Instead, I'm fairly certain that she is building me a kite — the same as last year, and the year before: the year before that we exchanged slingshots. All of which is fine by me. For we are champion kite-fliers who study the wind like sailors; my friend, more accomplished than I, can get a kite aloft when there isn't enough breeze to carry clouds.

Christmas Eve afternoon we scrape together a nickel and go to the butcher's to buy Queenie's traditional gift, a good gnawable beef bone. The bone, wrapped in funny paper, is placed high in the tree near the silver star. Queenie knows it's there. She squats at the foot of the tree staring up in a trance of greed: when bedtime arrives she refuses to budge. Her excitement is equaled by my own. I kick the covers and turn my pillow as though it were a scorching summer's night. Somewhere a rooster crows: falsely, for the sun is still on the other side of the world.

"Buddy, are you awake?" It is my friend, calling from her room, which is next to mine; and an instant later she is sitting on my bed holding a candle. "Well, I can't sleep a hoot," she declares. "My mind's jumping like a jack rabbit. Buddy, do you think Mrs. Roosevelt will serve our cake at dinner?" We huddle in the bed, and she squeezes my hand I-love-you. "Seems like your hand used to be so much smaller. I guess I hate to see you grow up. When you're grown up, will we still be friends?" I say always. "But I feel so bad, Buddy. I wanted so bad to give you a bike. I tried to sell my cameo Papa gave me. Buddy —" she hesitates, as though embarrassed —"I made you another kite." Then I confess that I made her one, too; and we laugh. The candle burns too short to hold. Out it goes, exposing the starlight, the stars spinning at the window like a visible caroling that slowly, slowly daybreak silences. Possibly we doze; but the beginnings of dawn splash us like cold water: we're up, wide-eyed and wandering while we wait for others to waken. Quite deliberately my friend drops a kettle on the kitchen floor. I tap-dance in front of closed doors. One by one the household emerges, looking as though they'd like to kill us both; but it's Christmas, so they can't. First, a gorgeous breakfast: just everything you can imagine — from flapjacks and fried squirrel to hominy grits and honey-in-the-comb. Which puts everyone in a good humor except my friend and me. Frankly, we're so impatient to get at the presents we can't eat a mouthful.

Well, I'm disappointed. Who wouldn't be? With socks, a Sunday school shirt, some handkerchiefs, a hand-me-down sweater and a year's subscription to a religious magazine for children. *The Little Shepherd.* It makes me boil. It really does.

My friend has a better haul. A sack of Satsumas, that's her best present. She is proudest, however, of a white wool shawl knitted by her married sister. But she *says* her favorite gift is the kite I built her. And it *is* very beautiful; though not as beautiful as the one she made me, which is blue and scattered with gold and green Good Conduct stars; moreover, my name is painted on it, "Buddy."

"Buddy, the wind is blowing."

The wind is blowing, and nothing will do till we've run to a pasture below the house where Queenie has scooted to bury her bone (and where, a winter hence, Queenie will be buried, too). There, plunging through the healthy waist-high grass, we unreel our kites, feel them twitching at the string like sky fish as they swim into the wind. Satisfied, sun-warmed, we sprawl in the grass and peel Satsumas and watch our kites cavort. Soon I forget the socks and hand-me-down sweater. I'm as happy as if we'd already won the fifty-thousand-dollar Grand Prize in that coffee-naming contest.

"My, how foolish I am!" my friend cries, suddenly alert, like a woman remembering too late she has biscuits in the oven. "You know what I've always thought?" she asks in a tone of discovery, and not smiling at me but a point beyond. "I've always thought a body would have to be sick and dying before they saw the Lord. And I imagined that when He came it would be like looking at the Baptist window: pretty as colored glass with the sun pouring through, such a shine you don't know it's getting dark. And it's been a comfort: to think of that shine taking away all the spooky feeling. But I'll wager it never happens. I'll wager at the very end a body realizes the Lord has already shown Himself. That things as they are" — her hand circles in a gesture that gathers clouds and kites and grass and Queenie pawing earth over her bone — "just what they've always seen, was seeing Him. As for me, I could leave the world with today in my eyes."

From

The Cat Who Came for Christmas

Cleveland Amory

Cleveland Amory is an animal person. He founded the Fund for Animals and is president of the New England Anti-Vivisection Society. But he does not have any animals to call his own, because, as he says, he is not home enough to take care of one. Until one Christmas Eve when he rescues a stray cat that he welcomes into his home — and into his heart.

*T*o anyone who has ever been owned by a cat, it will come as no surprise that there are all sorts of things about your cat you will never, as long as you live, forget.

Not the least of these is your first sight of him or her.

That my first sight of mine, however, would ever be memorable seemed, at the time, highly improbable. For one thing, I could hardly see him at all. It was snowing, and he was standing some distance from me in a New York City alley. For another thing, what I did see of him was extremely unprepossessing. He was thin and he was dirty and he was hurt.

The irony is that everything around him, except him, was beautiful. It was Christmas Eve, and although no one outside of New York would believe it on a bet or a Bible, New York City can, when it puts its mind to it, be beautiful. And that Christmas Eve some years ago was one of those times.

The snow was an important part of it — not just the snow, but the fact it was still snowing, as it is supposed to but rarely does over Christmas. And the snow was

beginning to blanket, as at least it does at first, a mult-
itude of such everyday New York sins as dirt and
noise and smells and potholes. Combined with this, the
Christmas trees and the lights and decorations inside
the windows, all of which can often seem so ordinary in
so many other places, seemed, in New York that night,
with the snow outside, just right.

I am not going so far as to say that New York that
night was O Little Town of Bethlehem, but it was at least
something different from the kind of New York Christmas
best exemplified by a famous Christmas card sent out by
a New York garage that year to all its customers. "Merry
Christmas from the boys at the garage," that card said.
"Second Notice."

For all that, it was hardly going to be, for me, a Merry
Christmas. I am no Scrooge, but I am a curmudgeon
and the word *merry* is not in the vocabulary of any self-
respecting curmudgeon you would care to meet — on
Christmas or any other day. You would be better off
with a New York cabdriver, or even a Yankee fan.

There were other reasons why that particular Christmas had little chance to be one of my favorites. The fact
that it was after seven o'clock and that I was still at my
desk spoke for itself. The anti-cruelty society which I
had founded a few years before was suffering growing pains — frankly, it is still suffering them — but at
that particular time, they were close to terminal. We
were heavily involved in virtually every field of animal

work, and although we were doing so on bare subsistence salaries — or on no salary at all for most of us — the society itself was barely subsisting. It had achieved some successes, but its major accomplishments were still in the future.

And so, to put it mildly, was coin of the realm. Even its name, The Fund for Animals, had turned out to be a disappointment. I had, in what I had thought of as a moment of high inspiration, chosen it because I was certain that it would, just by its mention, indicate we could use money. The name had, however, turned out not only not to do the job but to do just the opposite. Everybody thought that we already had the money.

Besides the Fund's exchequer being low that Christmas Eve, so was my own. My writing career, by which I had supported myself since before you were born, was far from booming. I was spending so much time getting the Fund off the ground that I was four years behind on a book deadline and so many months behind on two magazine articles that, having run out of all reasonable excuses, one of the things I had meant to do that day was to borrow a line from the late Dorothy Parker and tell the editor I had really tried to finish but someone had taken the pencil.

As for my personal life, that too left something to be desired. Recently divorced, I was living in a small apartment, and although I was hardly a hermit — I had a goodly choice of both office parties and even friends' parties to go to that evening — still, this was not going to be what Christmas is supposed to be. Christmas is, after all, not a business holiday or a friends' holiday, it is a family holiday. And my family, at that point, consisted of one beloved daughter who lived in Pittsburgh and had a perfectly good family of her own.

On top of it all, there was a final irony in the situation. Although I had had animals in my life for as far back as I could remember, and indeed had had them throughout my marriage — and although I was working on animal problems every day of my life — I had not a single creature to call my own. For an animal person, an animalless home is no home at all. Furthermore, mine, I was sure, was fated to remain that way. I travelled on an average of more than two weeks a month, and was away from home almost as much as I was there. For me, an animal made even less sense than a wife. You do not, after all, have to walk a wife.

I had just turned from the pleasant task of watching the snow outside to the unpleasant one of surveying the bills when the doorbell rang. If there had been anyone else to answer it, I would have told them to say to whoever it was that we already gave at home. But there was no one, so I went myself.

The caller was a snow-covered woman whom I recognized as Ruth Dwork. I had known Miss Dwork for many years. A former schoolteacher, she is one of those people who, in every city, make the animal world go round. She is a rescuer and feeder of everything from dogs to pigeons and is a lifetime soldier in what I have called the Army of the Kind. She is, however, no private soldier in that army — she makes it too go round. In fact, I always called her Sergeant Dwork.

"Merry Christmas, Sergeant," I said. "What can I do you for?"

She was all business. "Where's Marian?" she asked. "I need her." Marian Probst, my longtime and longer-suffering assistant, is an experienced rescuer, and I knew Miss Dwork had, by the very look of her, a rescue in progress. "Marian's gone," I told her. "She left about five-thirty, saying something about some people having Christmas Eve off. I told her she was a clock-watcher, but it didn't do any good."

Sergeant Dwork was unamused. "Well, what about Lia?" she demanded. Lia Albo is national coordinator of the Fund for Animals and an extremely expert rescuer. She, however, had left before Marian on — what else? — another rescue.

Miss Dwork was obviously unhappy about being down to me. "Well," she said, looking me over critically but trying to make the best of a bad bargain, "I need someone with long arms. Get your coat."

As I walked up the street with Sergeant Dwork, through the snow and biting cold, she explained that she had been trying to rescue a particular stray cat for almost a month, but that she had had no success. She had, she said, tried everything. She had attempted to lure the cat into a Hav-a-Heart trap but, hungry as he was and successful as this method had been in countless other cases, it had not worked with this cat. He had simply refused to enter any enclosure that he could not see his way out of. Lately, she confessed, she had abandoned such subtleties for a more direct approach. And, although she had managed to get the cat to come close to the rail fence at the end of the alley, and even to take bite-sized chunks of cheese from her outstretched fingers, she had never been able to get him to come quite close enough so that she could catch him. When she tried, he would jump away, and then she had to start all over the each-time-ever-more-difficult task of trying to win his trust.

However, the very night before, Sergeant Dwork informed me, she had come the closest she had ever come to capturing the cat. The time, she said, as he devoured the cheese, he had not jumped away but had stood just where he was — nearer than he had ever been but still maddeningly just out of reach. Good as this news was, the bad news was that Miss Dwork now felt that she was operating against a deadline. The cat had been staying in the basement of the apartment building, but the superintendent of the building had now received orders to get rid of it before Christmas or face the consequences. And now the other workers in the building, following their super's orders, had joined in the war against the cat. Miss Dwork herself had seen someone, on her very last visit, throw something at him and hit him.

When we arrived at our destination, there were two alleyways. "He's in one or the other," Sergeant Dwork whispered. "You take that one, I'll take this." She disappeared to my left and I stood there, hunched in my coat with the snow falling, peering into the shaft of darkness and having, frankly, very little confidence in the whole plan.

The alley was a knife cut between two tall buildings filled with dim, dilapidated garbage cans, mounds of snowed-upon refuse, and a forbidding grate. And then, as I strained my eyes to see where, amongst all this dismal debris, the cat might be hiding, one of the mounds of refuse suddenly moved. It stretched and shivered and turned to regard me. I had found the cat.

As I said, that first sight was hardly memorable. He looked less like a real cat than like the ghost of a cat. Indeed, etched as he was against the whiteness of the snow all around him, he was so thin that he would have looked completely ghostlike, had it not been for how pathetically dirty he was. He was so dirty, in fact, that it was impossible even to guess as to what color he might originally have been.

When cats, even stray cats, allow themselves to get

like that, it is usually a sign that they have given up. This cat, however, had not. He had not even though, besides being dirty, he was wet and he was cold and he was hungry.

And, on top of everything else, you could tell by the kind of off-kilter way he was standing that his little body was severely hurt. There was something very wrong either with one of his back legs or perhaps with one of his hips. As for his mouth, that seemed strangely crooked, and he seemed to have a large cut across it.

But, as I said, he had not given up. Indeed, difficult as it must have been for him from that off-kilter position, he proceeded, while continuing to stare at me unwaveringly, to lift a front paw — and, snow or no snow, to lick it. Then the other front paw. And, when they had been attended to, the cat began the far more difficult feat of hoisting up, despite whatever it was that was amiss with his hips, first one back paw and then the other. Finally, after finishing, he did what seemed to me completely incredible — he performed an all-four-paw, ears-laid-back, straight-up leap. It looked to me as if he was, of all things in such a situation, practicing his pounce.

An odd image came to my mind — something, more years ago than I care to remember, that my first college tennis coach had drilled into our team about playing three-set matches. "In the third set," he used to say, "extra effort for ordinary results." We loathed the saying and we hated even more the fact that he made us, in that third set, just before receiving serve, jump vigorously up and down. He was convinced that this unwonted display would inform our opponents that we were fairly bursting with energy — whether that was indeed the fact or not. We did the jumping, of course, because we had to, but all of us were also convinced that we were the only players who ever had to do such a silly thing. Now when I see, without exception, every top tennis player in the world bouncing like cork into the third set, I feel like a pioneer and very much better about the whole thing.

And when I saw the cat doing his jumping, I felt better too — but this time, of course, about him. Maybe he was not as badly hurt as at first I had thought.

In a moment I noticed that Sergeant Dwork, moving quietly, had rejoined me. "Look at his mouth," she whispered. "I told you they have declared war on him!"

Ours was to be a war too — but one not against, but for, the cat. As Sergeant Dwork quietly imparted her battle plan, I had the uneasy feeling that she obviously regarded me as a raw recruit, and also that she was trying to keep my duties simple enough so that even a mere male could perform them. In any case, still whispering, she told me she would approach the fence with the cheese cubes, with which the cat was by now thoroughly familiar, in her outstretched hand, and that, during this period, I apparently should be crouching down behind

179

her but nonetheless moving forward with her. Then, when she had gotten the cat to come as close as he would, she would step swiftly aside and I, having already thrust my arms above her through the vertical bars of the fence, was to drop to my knees and grab. The Sergeant was convinced that the cat was so hungry that, at that crucial moment, he would lose enough of his wariness to go for the bait — and the bite — which would seal his capture.

Slowly, with our eyes focused on our objective, we moved out and went over the top. And just as we did so, indeed as I was crouching into position behind Sergeant Dwork, I got for the first time a good look at the cat's eyes peering at us. They were the first beautiful thing I ever noticed about him. They were a soft and lovely and radiant green.

As Sergeant Dwork went forward, she kept talking reassuringly to the cat, meanwhile pointedly removing the familiar cheese from her pocket and making sure he would be concentrating on it rather than the large something looming behind her. She did her job so well that we actually reached our battle station at almost the exact moment when the cat, still proceeding toward us, albeit increasingly warily, was close enough to take his first bite from the Sergeant's outstretched hand.

That first bite, however, offered us no chance of success. In one single incredibly quick but fluid motion, the cat grabbed the cheese, wolfed it down, and sprang back.

Our second attempt resulted in exactly the same thing. Again the leap, the grab, the wolf, and the backward scoot. He was simply too adept at the game of eat and run.

By this time I was thoroughly convinced that nothing would come of the Sergeant's plan. But I was equally convinced that we had somehow to get that cat. I wanted to get over that fence and go for him.

The Sergeant, of course, would have none of such foolhardiness, and, irritated as this made me, I knew she was right. I could never have caught the cat that way. The Sergeant was, however, thinking of something else. Wordlessly she gave me the sign of how she was going to modify her tactics. This time she would offer the cat not one but two cubes of cheese — one in each of her two outstretched hands. But this time, she indicated, although she would push her right hand as far as it would go through the fence, she would keep her left hand well back. She obviously hoped that the cat would this time attempt both bites before the retreat. Once more we went over the top — literally in my case, because I already had my hands through the fence over the Sergeant. And this time, just as she had hoped, the cat not only took the first bite but also went for that second one. And, at just that moment, as he was midbite, Sergeant Dwork slid to one side and I dropped to my knees.

As my knees hit the ground, my face hit the grate. But

I did not even feel it. For, in between my hands, my fingers underneath and my thumbs firmly on top, was cat. I had him.

Surprised and furious, he first hissed, then screamed, and finally, spinning right off the ground to midair, raked both my hands with his claws. Again I felt nothing, because by then I was totally engrossed in a dual performance — not letting go of him and yet somehow managing to maneuver his skinny, desperately squirming body, still in my tight grasp, albeit for that split second in just one hand, through the narrow apertures of the rail fence. And now his thinness was all-important because, skin and bones as he was, I was able to pull him between the bars.

Still on my knees, I raised him up and tried to tuck him inside my coat. But in this maneuver I was either overconfident or under-alert, because somewhere between the raising and the tucking, still spitting fire, he got in one final rake of my face and neck. It was a good one.

As I struggled to my feet, Sergeant Dwork was clapping her hands in pleasure, but obviously felt the time had now come to rescue me. "Oh," she said. "Oh dear. Your face. Oh my." Standing there in the snow, she tried to mop me with her handkerchief. As she did so, I could feel the cat's little heart racing with fear as he struggled to get loose underneath my coat. But it was to no avail.

I had him firmly corralled, and, once again, with both hands.

The Sergeant had now finished her mopping and become all Sergeant again. "I'll take him now," she said, advancing toward me. Involuntarily, I took a step backwards. "No, no, that's all right," I assured her. "I'll take him to my apartment." The Sergeant would have none of this. "Oh no," she exclaimed. "Why, my apartment is very close." "So is mine," I replied, moving the cat even farther into the depths of my coat. "Really, it's no trouble at all. And anyway, it'll just be for tonight. Tomorrow, we'll decide — er, what to do with him."

Sergeant Dwork looked at me doubtfully as I started to move away. "Well then," she said, "I'll call you first thing in the morning." She waved a mittened hand. "Merry Christmas," she said. I wished her the same, but I couldn't wave back.

Joe, the doorman at my apartment building, was unhappy about my looks. "Mr. Amory!" he exclaimed. "What happened to your face? Are you all right?" I told him that not only was I all right, he ought to have seen the other guy. As he took me to the elevator, he was obviously curious about both the apparent fact that I had no hands and also the suspicious bulge inside my coat. Like all good New York City doormen, Joe is the soul of discretion — at least from tenant to tenant — but he has a bump of curiosity which would rival Mt. Everest. He is also, however, a good animal man, and he had a good idea that whatever I had, it was something alive. Leaning his head toward my coat, he attempted to reach in. "Let me pet it," he said. "No," I told him firmly. "Mustn't touch." "What is it?" he asked. "Don't tell anyone," I said, "but it's a saber-toothed tiger. Undeclawed, too." "Wow," he said. And then, just before the elevator took off, he told me that Marian was already upstairs.

I had figured that Marian would be there. My brother and his wife were coming over for a drink before we all went out to a party, and Marian, knowing I would probably be late, had arrived to admit them and hold, so to speak, the fort.

I kicked at the apartment door. When Marian opened it, I blurted out the story of Sergeant Dwork and the rescue. She too wanted to know what had happened to my face and if I was all right. I tried the same joke I had tried on Joe. But Marian is a hard woman on old jokes. "The only 'other guy' I'm interested in," she said, "is in your coat." I bent down to release my prize, giving him a last hug to let him know that everything was now fine.

Neither Marian nor I saw anything. All we saw, before his paws ever hit the ground, was a dirty tan blur, which, crooked hips notwithstanding, literally flew around the apartment — seemingly a couple of feet off the ground and all the time looking frantically for an exit.

In the living room I had a modest Christmas tree.

Granted, it was not a very big tree — he was not, at that time, a very big cat. Granted, too, that this tree had a respectable pile of gaily wrapped packages around the base and even an animal figure attached to the top. Granted even that it was festooned with lights which, at rhythmic intervals, flashed on and off. To any cat, however, a tree is a tree and this tree, crazed as he was, was no exception. With one bound he cleared the boxes, flashed up through the branches, the lights, and the light cord and managed, somewhere near the top, to disappear again. "Now that's a good cat," I heard myself stupidly saying. "You don't have to be frightened. Nothing bad is going to happen to you here."

Walking toward the tree, I reached for where I thought he would be next, but it was no use. With one bound, he vanished down the far side and, flashing by my flailing arms, tried to climb up the inside of the fireplace. Fortunately the flue was closed, thus effectively foiling his attempt at doing a Santa Claus in reverse.

When he reappeared, noticeably dirtier than before, I was waiting for him. "Good boy," I crooned, trying to sound my most reasonable. But it was no use. He was gone again, this time on a rapid rampage through the bedroom — one which was in fact so rapid that not only was it better heard than seen but also, during the worst of it, both Marian and I were terrified that he might try to go through the window. When he finally materialized again in the hall, even he looked somewhat discouraged.

Maybe, I thought desperately, I could reason with him now. Slowly I backed into the living room to get a piece of cheese from the hors d'oeuvre tray. This, I was sure, would inform him that he was among friends and that no harm would befall him. Stepping back into the hall, I found Marian looking baffled. "He's gone," she said. "Gone," I said. "Gone where?" She shook her head and I suddenly realized that, for the first time in some time, there was no noise, there was no scurrying, there was no sound of any kind. There was, in fact, no cat.

We waited for a possible reappearance. When none was forthcoming, obviously we had no alternative but to start a systematic search. It is a comparatively small apartment and there are, or so Marian and I at first believed, relatively few hiding places. We were wrong. For one thing, there was a wall-long bookshelf in the living room, and this we could not overlook, for the cat was so thin and so fast that it was eminently feasible that he found a way to clamber up and wedge himself behind a stack of books on almost any shelf. Book by book, we began opening holes.

But he was not there. Indeed, he was not anywhere. We turned out three closets. We moved the bed. We wrestled the sofa away from the wall. We looked under the tables. We canvassed the kitchen. And here, although it is such a small kitchen that it can barely accommodate two normal-sized adults at the same time, we opened every cupboard, shoved back the stove, peered into the microwave, and even poked about in the tiny space under the sink.

At that moment, the doorbell rang. Marian and I looked at each other — it had to be my brother and his wife, Mary. My brother is one of only three men who went into World War II as a private and came out as a colonel in command of a combat division. He was, as a matter of fact, in the Amphibious Engineers, and made some fourteen opposed landings against the Japanese. He had also since served as deputy director of the CIA. A man obviously used to crises, he took one look at the disarray of the apartment. In such a situation, my brother doesn't talk, he barks. "Burglars," he barked. "It looks like a thorough job."

I explained to him briefly what was going on — and that the cat had now disappeared altogether. Not surprisingly, while Mary sat down, my brother immediately assumed command. He demanded to know where we had not looked. Only where he couldn't possibly go, I explained, trying to hold my ground. "I don't want theories," he barked. "Where *haven't* you looked?" Lamely, I named the very top shelves of the closet, the inside of the oven, and the dishwasher. "Right," he snapped, and advanced on first the closets, then the oven, and last the dishwasher. And, sure enough, at the bottom of the latter, actually curled around the machinery and wedged into the most impossible place to get to in the entire apartment, was the cat. "Ha!" said my brother, attempting to bend down and reach him.

I grabbed him from behind. I was not going to have my brother trust his luck with one more opposed landing. Bravely, I took his place. I was, after all, more expendable.

Actually, the fact was that none of us could get him out. And he was so far down in the machinery, even he couldn't get himself out. "Do you use it?" my brother demanded. I shook my head. "Dismantle it," he barked once more. Obediently, I searched for screwdriver, pliers, and hammer and, although I am not much of a mantler, I consider myself second to no one, not even my brother, as a dismantler. My progress, however, dissatisfied my brother. He brushed me aside and went over the top himself. I made no protest — with the dishwasher the Amphibious Engineer was, after all, at least close to being in his element.

When my brother had finished the job, all of us, Mary included, peered down at the cat. And, for the first time since my first sight of him in the alley, he peered back. He was so exhausted that he made no attempt to move, although he was now free to do so. "I would like to make a motion," Marian said quietly. "I move that we leave him right where he is, put out some food and water and a litter pan for him — and leave him be. What he needs now is peace and quiet."

The motion carried. We left out three bowls — of water, of milk, and of food — turned out all the lights, including the Christmas lights, and left him.

That night, when I got home, I tiptoed into the apartment. The three bowls were just where we had left them — and every one of them was empty. There was, however, no cat. But this time I initiated no search. I simply refilled the dishes and went to bed. With the help of a sergeant, a colonel, and Marian, I now had, for better or for worse, for a few days at least, a Christmas cat.

I awoke early the next morning — the earliest I could remember since the Christmas mornings of my childhood. In those days my brother and sister and I were allowed whenever we woke up to open our stockings with their presents inside, all individually wrapped and dutifully stuffed by Santa Claus. It was one of the few times I envied my sister. She not only still believed in Santa Claus — my brother and I were under threat of receiving no stocking at all if we attempted to persuade her otherwise — but she was also given a grown-up girl's stocking that was more than twice as long as ours and thus held many more presents. Liberation came early to our family.

In any case, my standing Christmas morning record for those days was 4 A.M. On my first Christmas with the cat, I did not break that record, but I came pretty close. Nonetheless, I decided to get up immediately and conduct a search for him. But, as I sat sleepily up in bed, I saw immediately that there would be no need for this. For, only a few feet from my bed, standing in almost exactly the same position he was in the first time I ever saw him, and looking straight at me in almost exactly the same way, was the cat.

He had evidently been standing like that for some time, waiting for some signs of life from me. Now, seeing same, he spoke. "Aeiou," he said. "Ow yourself," I replied; "Merry Christmas." I reminded him that he was supposed to say "Meow." "Aeiou," he repeated. Obviously, he was not very good at consonants, but he was terrific at vowels.

As I got out of bed and walked close by him on my way to replenish his bowls, I noticed that he made no attempt to move away. Neither did he after he had finished eating and drinking. He just stood for a moment or two, licking and contemplating things. Then, slowly and solemnly, he began a tour of the apartment. When he went back into the bedroom, I followed him. In the corner, between the two windows, he paused and looked back at me. "Aeiou," he remarked once more. Obviously he wanted to get up on the windowsill and look out. And, equally obviously, this time he required some assistance, although the night before he had managed the same jump without any assistance — and at about thirty miles an hour.

I went over and lifted him. He looked around at me as

I touched him but otherwise did nothing. Instead, after a moment, he continued his slow, solemn tour, this time of the windowsill. He spent some time looking down on the street below and out at the snow-covered Central Park. Then he proceeded to jump across to the next window, which opens on a small balcony. This he regarded with such special interest that for some time he lay down, quietly moving his tail back and forth. He had, clearly, seen pigeons. Finally, he jumped down again and went back into the living room.

Once more I followed him and, for the very first time since I had seen him, he stretched out full length. Then he rolled over, put his head half under his shoulder and looked at me, meanwhile once again quietly moving his tail. Cats talk with their tails, and no cat ever expressed himself more clearly. "I'll take it," he was saying, in exactly the way a prospective new tenant, who had just made a complete tour of the premises, would agree to a lease. Satisfied, I went back to bed.

At about eight o'clock, the telephone rang. I could not believe anyone would call so early on Christmas morning. It was, as I might have guessed, Sergeant Dwork. "Merry Christmas," she said. "How's our cat?" "Fine," I replied, "just fine." I did my best to conceal the fact that, even at that stage of my life with the cat, I was not entirely happy with the "our." Apparently, I succeeded, because Sergeant Dwork went into high gear. "I've got great news," she said. "I have a woman who wants him."

191

"Terrific," I said. I did not, however, say this with enthusiasm, something Sergeant Dwork must have sensed,
because she quickly added, "I know her and she'll give
it a great home."

I told her I was sure she would. "But the thing is," Miss
Dwork continued, "she wants it right away. She wants it
as a Christmas present for her daughter. They lost their
own, you know."

I didn't, of course, but I tried to mobilize, if not enthusiasm, at least acquiescence. When could they come
and see it? Perhaps in the afternoon?

"Oh, no." Sergeant Dwork sounded shocked. "Not this
afternoon. This morning. Right now. In fact, she's already on the way to your apartment. Her name, by the
way, is Mrs. Wills."

"Whoa," I told her sternly. "Not so fast." I glanced to
where the cat had settled himself at ease in the living
room. "He's so dirty," I said, "and it seems so awful to
move him again, just when he's beginning to . . ."

But Sergeant Dwork cut me off. "Nonsense," she said.
"The sooner the better. If he makes himself too much at
home with you — and you get too fond of him," and here
a distinctly disturbing note crept into her voice, "well, it
will be just that much harder for both of you when you
do give him up. And, remember, you yourself admitted
that a permanent animal made no sense at all for you,
with the amount of time you're away and everything."

What she said, of course, did make sense, and I admitted as much. "Okay," I said, "I'll see Mrs. Wills. I'll call you afterward to let you know if she likes him."

As I hung up the phone, however, I could not look at the cat, although I could feel he was looking at me. Instead, I turned my head and looked out the window.

In short order, the doorbell rang. Mrs. Wills was a nice woman, but she was also a formidable one, and I am not at my best with formidable women early in the morning. Quickly, I realized, however, that I was perhaps being unfair — one thing which made her seem so formidable was that she was carrying a large cat carrier.

"I'm sorry to be so early," she said briskly, as, in all senses of the phrase, she moved in, "but I wanted it for . . ."

"I know," I said, "for a Christmas present for your daughter." I turned to gesture toward the cat. But there was, of course, no cat.

"That's funny," I hedged. "He was here just a second ago." I looked around nervously. The thought of another search such as the one the night before and watched by Mrs. Wills had all the appeal of an IRS audit. Mrs. Wills looked around.

"Whatever happened in here?" she asked. "It looks as if you've been bombed. Did the cat . . . ?"

I had of course completely forgotten the total disarray of the apartment. "Oh the cat," I repeated, attempting a light laugh. "Oh no. It wasn't the cat. It was my brother.

You see, my brother was here last night and we were looking for a book we couldn't find. My brother is a great reader, you know."

In explanations like that, one always adds one ridiculous note. Mrs. Wills' eyebrows rose slightly, as she surveyed the contents of the living room closet, which were still strewn across the foyer floor. "Hmmm," she said.

I asked her if I could get her some coffee. She shook her head. She obviously wanted only that for which she had come.

There was nothing to do but bite the bullet. "Here, boy," I boldly called, feeling not only idiotic, but knowing full well that the odds against his even being curious enough to acknowledge such a call, let alone come to it, especially with a stranger there, were astronomical. Nonetheless, I moved around the room, continuing my call while ostensibly straightening things but actually surreptitiously looking for him. Finally, just as Mrs. Wills had begun to tap her foot meaningfully, I maneuvered myself into the position I had first wanted to be in — i.e., pretending to straighten the rug by the sofa but actually looking underneath it. And there, sure enough, at the very back, against the wall, crouched and rigid, was the cat. "Oh!" I exclaimed, getting down on my hands and knees. "There he is! In his favorite place!"

Reluctantly, Mrs. Wills, too, assumed the position. "I can't see a thing," she complained. "Well," I volunteered, "I'll get a flashlight."

When I returned and shone the light upon him, his eyes glowed. The rest of him, however, had the look of a cornered hyena. "Oh," said Mrs. Wills. "Oh my. He's so wild-looking." Oh, don't worry about that," I assured her. "He's just a little surprised."

"And he's so *dirty*," she went on. "Well," I answered stiffly, "remember, he's been a stray. On the street. He can be cleaned up in no time."

But the inspection was not finished yet. "Why is he crouched so crookedly like that?" she wanted to know. "Is there something wrong with him?"

"Oh that's nothing," I assured her. "He sometimes even stands like that. I'm sure it can be fixed. And anyway, remember, he's not really himself. He's nervous with both of us looking at him like this."

Mrs. Wills, however, was by now relentless. "There's something wrong with his mouth," she observed.

"He's got a cut," I replied. "A very little cut. Really just a tiny cut."

She maneuvered herself upwards and returned to her chair. "Oh dear," she said, as if talking to herself. "I really don't know. Now that I've seen him I'm really not sure. I suppose I could try it. But Jennifer is just a little girl and this cat is going to take an awful lot of work."

I told her that I didn't think it would be that much. I had a suggestion for her. Why didn't she let me get him cleaned up and quieted down and then she could make her decision? I had in mind at least a couple of days.

The idea appealed to her — but not the timing. It had, apparently, to be a Christmas cat or no cat at all. She consulted her wristwatch. "I'll come back after church," she decided. "I'll leave the carrier here."

So, I reflected, that was that. I had at least tried to do what I thought would, in the long run, be the best thing for the cat. And while I realize that I could have acted a good deal more enthusiastic about the final outcome, the problem was that I just didn't feel very enthusiastic.

In any case, now there was nothing for it — Christmas morning or no Christmas morning — but to give him a bath. I went into the bathroom to procure soap and washcloths, over which I ran warm water, as well as a bath towel and even a bath mat.

When I returned to the living room, the cat was no longer under the sofa. He was back in the middle of the floor, just where, pre–Mrs. Wills, he had been before. It seemed to me that he understood exactly what the mat and the towel and all the rest of the paraphernalia were about, and knew exactly what I was about to do. But, at the same time, it also seemed that he simply could not believe I would do such a thing. His tail made an incredulous rat-tat. "Wash a cat!" he was exclaiming. "Boy, have I got my work cut out for me with this one!" He clearly felt that whatever my inexperience and limitations as a cat-keeper might be, surely even I would be familiar with the basics — and what could be more basic than the plain and simple fact that washing was his job, not mine?

He rose to his paws and looked up at me. I looked down at him. We were, in a sense, eyeball to eyeball — I at six feet three and he at six inches. Just the same, it was going to be, as it always is in such a confrontation, a question of who blinked first. And that would not, I had already determined, be me.

And it was not, really. All right, certain purists might cavil that I did not get right down to the job. They might even argue that I made a small blink. But they would be absolutely wrong and it would be utterly unfair to me to make any more of it than that. What actually happened is that, just at the moment when I was about to commence operations, and as his tail began to rat-tat ever more ominously, I suddenly decided, and quite on my own, having nothing to do with the fact that his back was slowly arching and he was making his ears flat, that it was entirely possible I didn't know enough about cat-washing, and should consult authorities.

Hastily, I laid down my washing materials, and repaired to the bookcase, where I had a whole shelf of books about cats. Like the other books, these were now in a state of sad disarray. Besides, I was looking for something very specific — not cats in general, but cat-washing. There were many references to the subject in the various book indexes, but as happens so often with thorny issues, there were also many disagreements. There were, in fact, two diametrically opposed schools of thought. One of these schools held that you should never, ever, wash a cat. The theory had it that not only do cats prefer to do the job themselves, but they also do it better than a human ever could, and furthermore, humans were likely to get soap in their eyes or in their fur, and this could be very bad for them. On the other hand, the other school believed that it was perfectly all right to wash your cat, and indeed was so essential that if you didn't, all sorts of bad things could happen to him.

I decided in view of the current situation, and weighing all the factors, to adhere to Theory Number Two, and thumbed through the books until I found one, entitled simply *You and Your Cat*, which seemed the most definitive on the subject. It was written by an English veterinarian, David Taylor, and, with high optimism, I began to read:

> The kitchen sink will probably make the best "bath." Before you start, make sure all the doors and windows are closed and that the room is free from cold drafts. Place a rubber mat in the sink to stop the cat from slipping.

So far, I decided, so good. The next paragraph, however, was another story:

198

If you think your cat is going to struggle, put it in a cotton sack, leaving only its head visible. Pour the shampoo into the sack and lower the cat and sack into the water. You can then massage the cat through the sack and form a lather.

Put the cat in a sack! Maybe, I thought, my brother and his regiment could achieve that objective, but that I alone could do so was highly doubtful. True, the cat was quiet that morning, but remembering the whirlwind of the night before, and not being an Amphibious Engineer myself, I foresaw the possibility of something on the order of, if not Gallipoli, at least Dunkirk.

Nothing, however, stopped the aquatic advance of Dr. Taylor:

Fill the sink with about 2–4 ins. of warm water. The water temperature should be as close to your cat's body heat of 101.4 F as possible. To lift the cat in, put one hand under its hind quarters and hold the scruff of its neck with the other. If your cat prefers, allow it to rest its front paws out of the water.

I was sure that the cat in question would not only so prefer, but would also seize the first opportunity to have a go with those paws at the alleged perpetrator of any such proposed ablutions. In any case, I had had enough. I replaced the book, went back to the cat, gathered up my materials, and with all the authority I could muster, spread the bath mat down beside him.

To my amazement, he promptly stepped over and stood upon it. Although I had taken the precaution of remaining standing for, if need be, a fast getaway, I soon realized that I had underestimated him. He had, apparently, made his point, but he had no intention of being churlish about it. If I was going to be fool enough to do somebody else's work — i.e., his — well then, so be it.

I could not resist him any longer. I knelt down beside him, took him in my arms and, ignoring how dirty he was, gave him a hug. I hugged so long that he let out a small and surprised-sounding "aeiou," but other than that, he did nothing. I'm sure it was the first hug, or sign of human affection, he had had for a very long time, if indeed ever in his life. After that, I began his bath and, without a sound or a hiss or a single pullback, he let me wash away to my heart's content — first gently and then, as I went through literally layers of dirt, harder and harder.

In good time, having made several trips to the bathroom to rinse out the cloths, I had scrubbed enough to make a startling discovery. Underneath all the dirt he was neither tan nor gray, the two colors which I had fully expected. He was, instead, white.

I could hardly contain my excitement — at which the now much cleaner tail for the first time in the operation, moved. "What color did you expect?" it was inquiring.

"Purple?" Almost in spite of myself, I heard myself answer him. "But you were so *dirty*," I protested. "White was the last color I expected."

After I had him reasonably presentable, at least for a first effort, and had towelled him dry, I stood up and inspected him. His green eyes with his by now relatively clean and pure white face made him look, for the first time, beautiful. Indeed to me, at that moment, he looked so beautiful that I had an urge simply to stare. I knew that few animals liked to be stared at, and that when a human being did so, they usually looked away. But he did not look away. He looked steadily back at me. Once more I bent and hugged him.

When the doorbell rang again, it was, of course, Mrs. Wills. But when I ushered her into the living room to review the subject at hand, the subject was, once again, not at hand. He had repaired, as usual, to his prepared position.

I handed her the flashlight. By now Mrs. Wills had grown accustomed to getting down on her hands and knees as part of the inspection tour, and she gamely turned on the flashlight and pushed her head under the sofa. "My God," she exclaimed suddenly, "he's white." Her head turned to me suspiciously. "Are you sure," she demanded, "that this is the same cat?" I assured her that it was, and indicated the pile of washcloths and towels lying on the hearth as proof. "I can't believe it," she said.

"It was nothing," I shrugged. "Just a matter of know-how and stick-to-itiveness. But you were right, Mrs. Wills. White cats do take an awful lot of work."

Mrs. Wills paid no attention. Instead, she was entirely concerned with making contact under the sofa. "Here, kitty, kitty," she called. She called it again — in fact, she called everything but kitchy-koo. Naturally, nothing worked. Mrs. Wills reached. The cat moved. Mrs. Wills reached again. The cat moved again. This stylized duet went on for some moments. Then Mrs. Wills pulled herself up and went over and sat down in a chair. She chose one, I noticed, directly across from the sofa. I sat down beside her.

"I've never had an animal in my life react to me like that," she said. "I've never even met one who wouldn't meet me halfway. I've always had a way with animals."

I told her that was just the trouble; he thought that she was going to take him away. Mrs. Wills ignored my bad pun. "I've never," she said firmly, "seen any animal *that* shy."

Once, I offered, I had had a schoolmaster who told us there was no such thing as being shy. He said that being shy was just being conceited, that you thought everybody was looking at you and thinking about you and of course they weren't.

Mrs. Wills now looked at me as if I had two heads. But she was still clearly considering the cat. "He's so pretty," she said. "Jennifer would love him."

It was time to pull out all the stops. Of course, I said, it might not be just shyness — you really never could tell. But on the other hand, it might be something else. I reminded her that white cats were, after all, albinos — and often deaf.

"Deaf!" she exclaimed. "You mean maybe he can't hear me calling?"

I told her that it was entirely possible — perhaps he could not.

For the first time Mrs. Wills looked doubtful. "I don't really know much about white cats," she said.

I moved in swiftly.

"It's not just the deafness," I told her; "it's the skin problems, too. White cats, you know, can have terrible skin trouble."

Now she looked positively uncomfortable. "Well," I went on relentlessly, "I'm sure it's not contagious. How old is Jennifer?"

"Ten," she replied worriedly.

"Well, I suppose she could wear gloves," I suggested. "Of course, skin problems can make a cat edgy. Fortunately, he isn't very large. But he certainly can be fierce. And he sure can swipe." I indicated the scratches on face and neck. "He really got me one awful one. Fortunately, he didn't get near my eyes. Does Jennifer wear glasses?"

Mrs. Wills' own eyes were now riveted on me. "It was nothing, of course," I said, "and Ruth Dwork was quick at staunching the blood." I paused. "Just the same, I don't think it would be wise, at least in the beginning, to leave Jennifer alone with him."

She looked back down at the bottom of the sofa. "But anyway," I went on, "he'll probably be at the vet most of the first several months anyway. You were so right about that crooked way he stands. He'll need at least one operation, for sure."

Mrs. Wills said nothing for a long while. Then a smile slowly started across her face. "Mr. Amory," she asked, "are you planning to keep this cat yourself?"

It was my turn to smile. "Why, Mrs. Wills," I said, "whatever gave you that idea?"

She got up and picked up the cat carrier. "A little bird told me," she said. I started to apologize for her trouble in having to come to the apartment twice. "Don't," she said. "And don't call Ruth Dwork. I want the fun of telling her how it all happened." She paused a last time. "I wish you all the luck in the world with your cat." She grinned and got in a last jab. "From what you've just told me about him," she said, "you're going to need it. Merry Christmas."